# Food and healthy eating

CURR.LINKS ages 5–7

Suzanne Kirk

# Credits

**Author**
Suzanne Kirk

**Editor**
Roanne Charles

**Assistant Editor**
Charlotte Ronalds

**Series designer**
Lynne Joesbury

**Designer**
Catherine Mason

**Illustrations**
Sarah Warburton

**Cover photographs**
© Nova Developments

**Photographic symbols**
Science © Ingram Publishing
Design & technology © Photodisc, Inc.

Published by Scholastic Ltd,
Villiers House,
Clarendon Avenue,
Leamington Spa,
Warwickshire
CV32 5PR
**Printed by Bell & Bain Ltd, Glasgow**
Text © Suzanne Kirk
© 2004 Scholastic Ltd
1 2 3 4 5 6 7 8 9 0   4 5 6 7 8 9 0 1 2 3

Visit our website at www.scholastic.co.uk

British Library Cataloguing-in-Publication Data
A catalogue record for this book is available from
the British Library.

ISBN 0-439-97123-3

The right of Suzanne Kirk to be identified as the Author of this work has been asserted by her in accordance with the Copyright, Designs and Patents Act 1988.

All rights reserved. This book is sold subject to the condition that it shall not, by way of trade or otherwise, be lent, hired out or otherwise circulated without the publisher's prior consent in any form of binding or cover other than that in which it is published and without a similar condition, including this condition, being imposed upon the subsequent purchaser.

No part of this publication may be reproduced, stored in a retrieval system, or transmitted, in any form or by any means, electronic, mechanical, photocopying, recording or otherwise, without the prior permission of the publisher. This book remains copyright, although permission is granted to copy those pages marked 'photocopiable' for classroom distribution and use only in the school which has purchased the book or by the teacher who has purchased the book and in accordance with the CLA licensing agreement. Photocopying permission is given for purchasers only and not for borrowers of books from any lending service.

**INTRODUCTION**

**GETTING STARTED**

**SECTION 1**
All kinds of food

**SECTION 2**
Tasting and eating foods

**SECTION 3**
Eat more fruit and vegetables

**SECTION 4**
Exercise

**SECTION 5**
Medicines

**SECTION 6**
Growing up

**DISPLAY IDEAS**

# Acknowledgements

**Photographs**
pages 5 and 53 © Photodisc, Inc.
pages 6, 11, 25, 36 and 45
© Nova Developments
pages 8 and 22 © SODA
pages 15, 19 and 36 © Ingram Publishing
page 51 © 2004/Harald Theissen/alamy.com
page 52 © 2004/Robert Llewellyn/alamy.com
page 56 © Corbis

# Introduction

*Food and healthy eating* provides suggestions and activities covering separate areas of the curriculum that as a whole, create an exciting and motivating topic to raise children's awareness of the responsibilities they have towards themselves as they grow up. The activities cover health issues, focusing primarily on the importance of a balanced diet, the need for exercise and the safe use of medicines. Children are introduced to the concept that eating a wide range of foods is essential for health, and are encouraged to increase their consumption of fruit and vegetables.

This book brings together aspects of science with design and technology, as well as the opportunity to develop the school's policy for PSHE. It will help you to present an interesting and relevant topic at Key Stage 1 over a number of weeks, encouraging children to focus on a healthy lifestyle as part of their daily life.

Generally, the activities in each section of *Food* follow on progressively. Sections 1 and 2 look at the range of foods available and involve observation and investigation of fruits and vegetables. The emphasis is on the importance of these foods in our diet. Section 3 includes planning, making and evaluating a fruit or vegetable dish. Section 4 is devoted to the need for exercise. Section 5 looks at the uses and dangers of medicines. Section 6 rounds off the topic with activities relating to growing up.

## What subject areas are covered?

This book covers the QCA science unit 2A, 'Health and growth', and design and technology unit 1C, 'Eat more fruit and vegetables'.

Almost all children are interested in food and undoubtedly have favourite things they like to eat. However, developing healthy eating habits has never been so important as today when there is such a range of products offered and advertised to children. Unsuitable foods with a high fat, salt or sugar content are readily available, and often chosen by children as snacks to be eaten throughout the day. Encouraging a sensible eating pattern with an emphasis on consuming more fruit and vegetables is important in ensuring the healthy development of a young child. Today's children are becoming less active in their daily lives with resulting health problems, including obesity. Discovering that regular exercise is enjoyable as well as important can promote good habits which continue throughout childhood and into adult life.

There are useful opportunities to show children how science relates to their everyday lives, particularly the part it plays in their personal health.

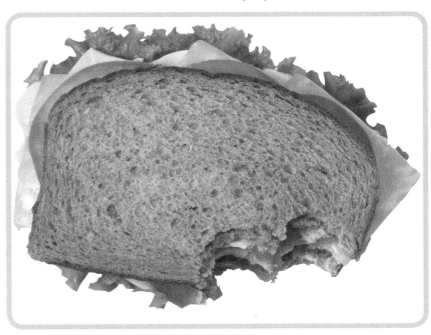
© Photodisc, Inc.

## Teaching specific subject areas through a topic

While it is important to distinguish between the separate subject areas of science and design and technology, natural links are extremely useful in relating one area of work with another. One subject focus can provide an opportunity to explore another field.

A carefully planned topic can meld together prescribed areas of the curriculum to create interesting learning experiences appropriate to the needs of the class. Topic-based work presents a whole picture, motivates children and encourages their enthusiasm.

# Getting started

Assess the children's experiences and attitudes as a whole towards food. Depending on location and other factors, the range of fruits and vegetables available might be quite limited or very extensive. Find out if there are supermarkets nearby with a vast range of products or only small shops with a restricted range. Do the children ever have the chance to see food growing? Is there a farm, orchard, nursery or market garden nearby?

Begin by making a collection of books, pictures, posters, video clips and so on about food and health issues relating to growing up. Try to find those that also include exercise and the safe use of medicines. Your local health centre might be able to help.

List possible experts who might be willing to share their experiences with the class, for example school meals staff; a children's nutritionist; a health adviser; parents and carers who work in food retail, grow vegetables or work as chefs or professional caterers.

This topic raises a number of potentially sensitive issues. Sensitivity towards the differences in family life among the children is important: be aware of economic, cultural and social differences. Avoid isolating children who have physical or health problems.

## Involving parents and carers

Involving parents and carers is a useful strategy and can be important in helping to motivate children during their topic work. Prepare a letter to parents and carers that outlines the areas of work their children are undertaking. Encourage them to take an interest and explain how they can become involved.

Advise parents and carers that there will be food tasting and simple food preparation activities. Ask permission for individuals to take part in these and request information relating to food allergies and cultural restrictions so that problems can be avoided. Encourage parents and carers to get in touch beforehand if they have any queries or concerns about this aspect of the topic.

Suggest that children will want to talk with their parents/carers about their learning and experiences, and perhaps practise their new-found skills with fruit and vegetable preparation under adult supervision. Where appropriate, request help from parents/carers with babies or toddlers. Point out that as the topic develops they might be asked simple questions relating to the growth and care of small children.

## Introducing the topic to children

Present this topic as an exciting project for both the children and yourself, with many different and interesting activities to look forward to. Explain that as the children grow up, looking after their bodies and keeping fit is very important. The science activities you have planned will show them how food, exercise and keeping safe will help them to enjoy healthy lives as children, grow into strong teenagers and develop into fit adults. Explain that some events will be especially enjoyable as there will be different foods to taste and physical exercises to take part in. As part of their work in design and technology, they will learn how to use tools to prepare special foods and interesting dishes.

## Starting points
Ask the children to tell you some of the things they do each day that they look forward to and enjoy. Highlight physical activities and meal times. Point out that, as well as being enjoyable in itself, eating and drinking every day provides energy to do the other things children enjoy. Explain to the children that they are growing up rapidly. Their bodies are gradually changing and they are learning new things every day.

## Scientific observation and investigation
The activities provide the children with opportunities for making and recording observations of different fruits and vegetables, looking closely at familiar examples and discovering new ones. Information collected during some of the activities is presented scientifically as charts. There are ideal opportunities to demonstrate how science relates to our personal everyday life, especially involving our health.

## Resources
Gather pictures, posters, advertising material, packaging, recipe cards and books, and so on relating to the following categories:
- children and adults involved in day-to-day activities
- popular foods
- a wide range of fruits and vegetables
- foods representing the main food groups
- stages in growing up – babies, young children, adults
- parent animals and their young.

Samples of these **foods** will be needed:
- a range of fruits and vegetables
- examples of salty, spicy, sweet, sour and savoury foods
- snack foods typically enjoyed by the children.

You will also need **tools and equipment** to use in preparing and tasting the foods:
- paper or plastic plates
- plastic bowls, beakers, fruit squeezers and graters
- serrated knives with rounded ends, small forks
- plastic table covering, chopping boards, waste containers
- kitchen paper, cling film, antibacterial wipes
- facility to cook food
- aprons.

Try to collect as many of these **other resources** as possible:
- equipment needed when caring for babies and toddlers (these can be in the form of toys)
- small items of PE equipment – soft balls, hoops, beanbags, and so on
- packaging from a range of different medicines including safety bottles and blister packs
- stories and poems about growing up, eating healthily, fruits and vegetables, exercise
- other printed resource material on the topic
- video clips of animals and their young, and babies and toddlers being cared for at home
- software for creating pictograms and bar charts
- still and video cameras.

Enlist the help of experts, such as a health worker, who will agree to visit and answer the children's questions; perhaps also a nutritionalist, nurse, chef, and parent or carer of a baby or toddler.
  To demonstrate the growth and development of fruits and vegetables as plants we use for food, try growing a tomato, potato or strawberry plant in a pot, and lettuces and radishes in a garden plot in the school grounds.

# Section 1 — All kinds of food

## FOCUS

**SCIENCE**
- our need for food and water
- popular foods
- different types of food

**DESIGN & TECHNOLOGY**
- the variety of fruit and vegetables
- examining fruits and vegetables
- developing sensory vocabulary

## ACTIVITY 1

### WE NEED FOOD AND WATER

**Learning objective**
To understand that humans and other animals need food and water to stay alive.

**Resources**
Images of adults engaged in a variety of purposeful activities, for example milkman, doctor, famous athlete, explorer; images of children involved in a variety of enjoyable activities; paper, pencils and crayons.

**Preparation**
Be aware of the need for sensitivity towards children with disabilities and illnesses or health conditions.

**Activity**
Discuss with the children some of the things they have done so far on this day. Point out that their bodies have been able to move about and walk around the school, perhaps moving in quite an energetic way during a PE lesson or at playtime. The children have been talking and laughing with each other, listening and learning. Their brains have been active as they make decisions, follow instructions and try to understand new things.

Explain that in order to do *all* these activities, even just sitting still and thinking, human bodies need to be provided with food and drink that keeps the body parts working and in the case of children, helps their bodies to grow.

# All kinds of food

Ask some children to tell the class what foods and drinks they have consumed so far today to keep their bodies in good working order. Talk about eating and drinking being important daily activities for all humans.

From this discussion, emphasise the fact that humans and all other animals need food and water even to stay alive. Without food and water, animals cannot survive. Although other animals require different types of food from humans, we all need water. You could put it in 'dramatic' terms: consuming food and water are absolutely vital for the children to continue living: to breathe, move, think and carry out everyday tasks.

Refer to the collection of images of children and adults. Together identify what each is doing, then explain that none of these tasks would be possible without our bodies being sustained by food and water.

## Recording
Ask the children to write or complete sentences stating the importance of food and drink relating to themselves, for example *I need food and drink to…* They could choose three or four activities they perform to write about and illustrate. To encourage a wide range of actions, suggest the children choose a school task, a playtime or vigorous activity and something that chiefly uses their brains, such as thinking of good ideas, reading, making a decision and planning an event.

Ask them to also write a statement to explain what would happen if any animal, including themselves, did not have food or drink.

## Differentiation
Children:
■ know that humans and other animals need food and water to stay alive, recording this by completing sentences and illustrations
■ know that humans and other animals need food and water to stay alive, recording this with sentences and illustrations
■ know that humans and other animals need food and water to stay alive, showing their understanding in sentences and illustrations.

## Plenary
Ask the children to remind each other of the importance of food and water in their daily lives; that food and water are necessary for their bodies to remain healthy and perform all kinds of activities, as well as to stay alive.

Perhaps point out that some children in some countries are not so fortunate as themselves and do not get enough food and water to keep their bodies healthy. Unfortunately these children become ill and often die before they can become adults.

## Display
Begin to build up a display about food with a statement as a heading: *We all need food and water to stay alive*. Add the children's recordings and the images of people engaged in physical and mental activities.

CURRICULUM LINKS ages 5–7: Food and healthy eating

All kinds of food

SCIENCE

## ACTIVITY 2

## WHAT FOODS DO WE EAT?

### Learning objective
To realise that there are many different foods that people like to eat.

### Resources
Pictures of a range of foods and dishes from advertising material, recipe books and magazines; paper, pencils and crayons, board or flip chart.

### Preparation
Decide how the children will be organised for their initial fact finding and discussion, ideally in pairs.

### Activity
Ask pairs of children to tell each other their favourite foods. Suggest they remember two foods that they both enjoy and two others (one for each child) that they have not tried or do not eat very often. Where necessary, remind the children to take turns to listen and speak, developing their discussion skills.

After about five minutes, bring the children together. First, point out that everyone has different tastes and that foods enjoyed by some people are disliked by others. Discourage unfavourable comments against unusual or unfamiliar foods. Then ask the pairs to share their discoveries with the rest of the class. As each pair provides information, write the names of the foods on the board. Comment on each food and group them where possible. Try to make a distinction between 'single' foods, such as bread, bananas and cheese, and those foods made up of several ingredients, such as pizza and curry. Ask individuals to talk about foods not recognised by everyone. Show pictures if available. Where foods have already been recorded, perhaps add ticks or tally bars to represent more than one choice.

When all the information has been collected, comment on the range of foods. Which foods are very popular and liked by most people? Which ones do only a few people enjoy? Compare the children's like of simple foods with that of combinations of foods.

### Recording
Ask the children to write and draw their favourite foods and those of their discussion partner, making simple comparisons. Perhaps provide some sentence frameworks: *My favourite food is ____. We both like ____. I like ____ but... I have never tried ____. I think I would like ____.*

### Differentiation
Children:
■ talk about their favourite foods, recording this with words and drawings
■ speak and listen when discussing favourite foods, making simple comparisons when recording
■ discuss their favourite foods with a partner, recording information in sentences and drawings and making useful comparisons.

### Plenary
Comment on the range of favourite foods among the children. Did they think there would be such a range of favourites? Perhaps most children like the same types of food. Remind the children that we all have different tastes and should be prepared to accept and respect others' likes and dislikes. Suggest the children talk with their families about favourite foods. They could find a picture or draw a picture of a dish, adding a sentence to their recording sheets: *My family's favourite food is ____.*

## Display
Use pictures of favourite foods to enhance a display of the children's work. Perhaps use a heading like *We all like different foods* and emphasise cultural diversity.

All kinds of food

## ACTIVITY 3

### DIFFERENT TYPES OF FOOD

SCIENCE

### Learning objective
To recognise different types of food and know that it is important to eat a range of foods to keep healthy.

### Resources
A range of basic foods from different food groups or items to represent foods, such as containers, packets, models and pictures: include examples of fruits, vegetables, breads, meat, fish (represented as fresh and in cans), milk, cheese, yogurt, different sorts of rice and pasta; photocopiable page 17; pencils and crayons.

### Preparation
Carefully select the different foods to use as examples so that the main food groups become evident.

### Activity
Remind the children of the previous activity where they talked about foods they like to eat. Comment on the range of different foods they discussed. Tell the children that you have some different types of food to show them and that these need to be sorted into groups.

Present the children with a selection of food items. Identify each one. Ask the children if they can see foods that are similar in any way and therefore could be grouped together. Help the children to recognise and group the fruits and the vegetables. Are they aware that sausages, bacon and chicken are all different types of meat? Do they know that there are many different types of bread? Point out that fish can be bought fresh as well as in cans.

Discuss the link between milk, cheese and yogurt and explain that these foods make a group of their own, usually referred to as dairy products. Talk about the many uses of rice and the different types of pasta.

Look at the various groups which the foods have been sorted into and explain that these are the main types of food we eat. Point out that it is important to eat a variety of foods from all the groups.

Next, introduce some other examples of foods and ask the children to decide which groups they belong in. Perhaps show a different type of canned fish, a picture of a joint of meat, a different type of bread, other varieties of fruits and vegetables.

© Nova Developments

CURRICULUM LINKS ages 5–7: Food and healthy eating

**1**

All kinds of food

Remind the children again that although we all have our favourite foods, we should eat a variety of foods every day in order to remain healthy and, in the case of children, to help their bodies to grow well.

### Recording
Read the names of the different types of food on photocopiable page 17 and point out the column headings. Ask the children to think carefully about how often they eat the foods listed and to show this information in the correct column, perhaps by using a tick. The children can illustrate the foods named to show their specific favourites of each type.

Explain that there might be a type of food which is not eaten much or at all in certain families, and that this can be a positive thing, reflecting variety and cultural diversity. Vegetarians, for example, do not eat meat and some families tend to eat more rice and pasta than other families.

Encourage the children to complete their recording with sentences that show they understand that eating a variety of foods is important for a healthy life. Talk to individual children as they complete their charts. Help them with their decisions if necessary, especially if they have religious restrictions or dietary problems.

### Differentiation
Children:
■ with help group basic foods and know that eating many different foods is important
■ recognise basic food types and sort different foods into groups, understanding that eating a wide range of foods is important for a healthy life
■ recognise basic food types, sort different foods into groups and explain why eating a wide range of foods is important.

### Plenary
Ask the children to consider their daily eating habits. Do they think they eat many different foods? Remind them that they should try to eat a wide range of foods to live and grow healthily.

### Display
Arrange pictures, packaging, models and books to show the different food groups. Title the display with, for example, *To live healthily we need to eat many different types of foods*.

## ACTIVITY 4
## FRUIT AND VEGETABLES

SCIENCE    DESIGN & TECHNOLOGY

### Learning objective
To know that there is a wide variety of fruit and vegetables.

### Resources
Some common types of fruits and vegetables and others less familiar to the children – depending on the season try to provide carrots or beetroot with leaves still attached, peas and beans in pods and so on; pictures, books and video clips showing fruits and vegetables growing; paper, pencils and crayons.

### Preparation
If possible, arrange a visit to a greengrocer's shop or market to see different types of fruit and vegetables, or a garden or allotment where fruits and vegetables can be seen growing.

## Activity
Display the fruits and vegetables. Remind the children of the previous activity, and establish to which groups these foods belong. Explain that there are many different types of fruits and vegetables and those they see here are just a few.

Let the children examine the specimens in turn and ask what they are called. Encourage comments on colours and textures, skin, stalks and leaves, and decide whether they are fruits or vegetables. Arrange them into the two groups.

Discuss fruits first. Ask the children which fruits they have seen growing, perhaps in gardens, when on holiday, or visiting a farm. Explain that many fruits grow on trees or bushes. Show pictures, and perhaps a video, to help the children associate the fruits with the parent plants. Talk about which fruits can be grown locally and which need hotter, sunnier weather found in other countries. Point out that some fruits, such as blackberries, can be found growing in the wild during the summer and autumn. However, warn the children that some wild fruits are poisonous to humans and must not be eaten. Remind them that they must not taste any parts of plants without the permission of a responsible adult.

Next, examine the vegetables and consider how they are different from the fruits. Children might comment on colour, taste and how they are prepared and eaten. Ask the children if they have seen vegetables growing. Perhaps relatives have gardens or allotments and children can describe what they have seen growing there. Discuss whether the vegetables in your collection grow below or above the ground. Talk about leaves, stalks, roots and pods. Show a video or pictures to demonstrate vegetables growing.

If possible, continue this activity by visiting a greengrocer's and/or an allotment or market garden where children can see fruits and vegetables growing.

Start a class list of fruits and vegetables to which children can add further examples as they discover them.

All kinds of food

## Recording
Ask the children to choose a fruit and a vegetable to examine, then make careful drawings of them. Talk about providing a heading and show how to add information to illustrations by writing labels to identify such things as shiny yellow skin, small stalk, curly leaves, and so on.

Begin to build up a database of pictures and words to describe many of the examples of fruits and vegetables and perhaps their countries of origin.

## Differentiation
Children:
- recognise fruits and vegetables, describing some in labelled drawings
- identify a range of fruits and vegetables from around the world, recording some with accurate drawings and relevant labelling
- understand that there is a wide variety of fruits and vegetables from around the world, recording examples with accurate drawings and detailed labelling.

## Plenary
Remind the children of the wide range of fruits and vegetables they have discovered, some of which grow in this country and others that are brought to the shops from other countries. Did they know there were so many different

CURRICULUM LINKS ages 5–7: Food and healthy eating

**All kinds of food**

types? Point out that some fruits and vegetables have been experienced at first hand by looking and touching, while information about others has been discovered from books, pictures or video clips. Suggest the children make a book of their own at home to show some examples of fruits and vegetables. Encourage them to find pictures or make drawings, and add headings and labels.

### Display
Begin a display devoted to fruits and vegetables. Use diagrams and models as well as the children's work. The children could cut out shapes of fruits and vegetables to make a border and use modelling clay to make models.

SCIENCE    DESIGN & TECHNOLOGY

## ACTIVITY 5
## GROUPING FRUITS AND VEGETABLES

### Learning objective
To compare and group fruits and vegetables, considering appearance, texture and scent.

### Resources
Fruits and vegetables, ideally including types not previously examined by the children; paper.

### Preparation
Make a vocabulary list of words to describe the colours, shapes and textures of fruits and vegetables.

### Activity
Display a collection of fruits. Ask the children if they can suggest any similarities between the examples. At first they might choose to talk about the colours, so spend some minutes arranging the fruits into colour groups. Decide what to do with fruits showing more than one colour, such as apples. They could be grouped separately or included in one of the main groups. Perhaps try arranging a colour line where colours blend from one to another.

Discuss the shapes of the fruits. Decide if they can easily be sorted according to shape. Use words such as *round, long, pointed, oval, curved*, and so on.

Next, encourage the children to handle the fruits gently and to describe their textures. Talk about skin and peel, use vocabulary such as *soft, hairy, rough, smooth, shiny, tough, delicate, wrinkled, dimpled*. Regroup the fruits according to their textures.

As the children examine the fruits they might begin to notice their scents. Suggest they sniff the fruits and decide if any are similar in the way they smell. Find out if all the fruits have a scent. Perhaps sort the fruits into those with a strong scent and those with a delicate scent.

Let the children know that they will not be tasting the fruits and vegetables at this stage.

Now show the children some fresh vegetables and identify them. The children's experience of sorting fruit can determine the procedure. Consider colour, shape, texture and scent. Make some comparisons with the fruits. Are the predominant colours different? Is there a greater range of shapes? Are there characteristic fruity scents that are different from the scents of vegetables?

### Recording
Provide pairs of children with two different fruits or two different vegetables, and ask them to talk about the similarities and differences in appearance, texture and scent. Then ask them to draw each specimen and write notes or sentences to explain what they have discovered. Refer them to the vocabulary list.

## Differentiation
Children:
- recognise differences between some fruits and vegetables, recording observations with drawings and words
- make relevant observations when comparing and grouping different fruits and vegetables, recording these with careful drawings and notes
- recognise a range of differences and similarities when observing fruits and vegetables, recording these accurately with observational drawings and notes, adding explanatory sentences.

All kinds of food

## Plenary
Emphasise the variety of fruits and vegetables available. Point out that each fruit or vegetable has its own distinctive characteristics, which is how we recognise it even though some might be quite similar in appearance, texture or scent. Ask the children to look out for stories about growing, harvesting and enjoying fruits and vegetables.

## Display
Continue to build up the fruits and vegetables display, adding new work by the children and further pictures.

# ACTIVITY 6
# INVESTIGATING FRUITS AND VEGETABLES

DESIGN & TECHNOLOGY

## Learning objective
To examine and compare the insides of fruits and vegetables.

## Resources
Fruits and/or vegetables that show contrasting interiors and perhaps are less familiar to the children, for example a pear rather than an apple to show a fruit with pips, a cherry or plum to show a stone, a lemon or satsuma rather than an orange to show segments, a banana; paper; pencils and crayons.

© Ingram Publishing

## Preparation
Decide whether to cut the fruits and vegetables as part of the activity or have them already prepared.

## Activity
Point out to the children that they have already examined fruits and vegetables closely from the outside, and that now they are going to investigate and compare the insides of some fruits and vegetables.

Show the children half of a pear cut lengthways. Identify the skin and the flesh. Point out the pips and explain that these are the seeds of the pear tree and are not eaten. Ask the children which other fruit looks very similar to this when cut in half.

Before cutting a stone fruit in half to reveal the interior, ask the children what they think the inside will be like. Talk about the colour of the flesh, the size of the stone, the thickness of

CURRICULUM LINKS ages 5–7: Food and healthy eating

**All kinds of food**

the skin and the amount of juice the fruit produces. Ask the children to suggest the part the stone plays in the life of the plant (which is a tree).

Demonstrate that it is possible to peel a citrus fruit with your fingers, as the skin is thicker than other fruits you have examined. Point out that the peel itself is not eaten. Show the children the segments of which the fruit is made up. Look for any pips and comment on the amount of juice. Ask the children what other fruits have a similar interior arrangement.

Slice a banana and ask the children in what ways it is similar to and different from other fruits examined.

Make sure the children appreciate which parts of each fruit is the food – the flesh, juice and sometimes the skin, and which parts are not usually eaten, such as apple pips and the skins of bananas and oranges.

If vegetables are available, investigate and compare the interiors of a potato, carrot and mild onion. Suggest the children carry out their own examination of peas and beans when they next eat these vegetables, and discuss the structure of a cabbage and lettuce. Identify skin, peel, any leaves and roots the plant might have. Point out the parts of the vegetables that provide the food.

### Recording
Provide pairs of children with slices or segments of two examples of fruits or vegetables and ask them to make detailed drawings with titles, labels and notes to show the similarities and differences. Some children might like to extend their recording to include a wider range of fruits/vegetables in order to make comparisons.

### Differentiation
Children:
■ talk about differences when examining the interiors of fruits and vegetables, recording this with titled and labelled drawings
■ identify a range of differences in the interiors of fruits and vegetables, recording observations with accurate drawings, titles and relevant labels

■ make useful comparisons between the interiors of different fruits and vegetables, recording differences and similarities in detail as drawings and with titles and notes.

### Plenary
Remind the children of the differences they observed when investigating the interiors of fruits and vegetables. Refer to the parts that provide food. Give simple clues and questions for the children to identify particular fruits and vegetables: *This fruit is small and round and often dark red. It has a stone inside. What could it be?*

### Display
Use the children's work to continue the display relating to fruits and vegetables.

All kinds of food

# Which foods do you eat and drink?

|  | every day | sometimes | never |
|---|---|---|---|
| bread |  |  |  |
| milk |  |  |  |
| fruit |  |  |  |
| vegetables |  |  |  |
| cheese |  |  |  |
| rice and pasta |  |  |  |
| meat and fish |  |  |  |

# Section 2

# Tasting and eating foods

## FOCUS

**SCIENCE**
- different tastes
- eating patterns
- the importance of fruits and vegetables in a balanced diet
- tasting and comparing fruits

**DESIGN & TECHNOLOGY**
- ways of preparing fruits and vegetables
- changes that occur when fruits and vegetables are cooked
- developing vocabulary

## ACTIVITY 1

### FAVOURITE TASTES

SCIENCE

### Learning objective
To collect information relating to food preferences and present the results graphically.

### Resources
Foods to represent contrasting tastes such as salty (crisps), sweet (chocolate), spicy (flavoured snack), sour (lemon), savoury (cheese); paper plates; plastic beakers; kitchen paper, cling film; pictogram software or a prepared chart and small pieces of coloured paper to represent each taste; pencils and crayons; board or flip chart.

### Preparation
Prepare the foods as necessary, arrange them on paper plates and keep them covered and cool until tasting takes place. Decide how the session will be organised, providing kitchen paper for the children to hold the food samples and beakers of water to sip between tastes. Ask the children to wash their hands thoroughly before the activity begins. Make sure you are aware of any food allergies children have.

### Activity
Explain to the children that during this activity they can taste some types of food, which is why they have washed their hands. Point out that only a small sample of each food is necessary for this tasting experience and no one needs to taste anything that they think they will not like. Talk to the children about taking the taste test seriously. Explain that it is an interesting and enjoyable way of collecting information, and if they find there are tastes they do not like, as well as ones they enjoy, they should react sensibly.

Begin by reminding the children that we need to eat every day; that eating is an important part of our daily lives. Without food and water we could not stay alive. Point out, however, that we all *enjoy* food too and eat many different types of food every day. (Refer to section 1, activity 2.) This could be because foods have quite different tastes which we like to try. Consider how uninteresting it would be if all foods tasted the same.

## Tasting and eating foods

Briefly talk about foods the children enjoy and encourage them to describe the tastes. They will probably use words to express personal enjoyment, such as *scrumptious*, *delicious*, *yummy* and so on. Explain that there are more accurate words to describe the tastes of different foods and list *salty, sweet, sour, spicy* and *savoury* on the board. Show the children a sample of a salty food, such as crisps. Talk about the taste beforehand so that they are prepared to recognise the saltiness. Suggest they eat each food slowly to experience the taste fully, perhaps closing their eyes. Ask the children to raise their hands if they liked the salty taste. Perhaps ask what other salty foods they like.

Allow the children to sip some water to remove the salty taste before trying the next food.

Present the children with another sample of food, perhaps something which is sweet. Again, ask what they expect the taste to be. After the tasting, ask if the food was very sweet. Have they tasted anything sweeter? Do all the children like sweet tasting foods?

Provide other foods with distinctive tastes to represent sour, spicy and savoury foods. Discuss the different tastes and find out which are popular with the children.

### Recording
After the children have tried the different foods, ask them to decide which is their favourite taste. Make sure the children can distinguish between their favourite type of taste (for example, sweet) and their favourite food (for example, chocolate). Explain that to record the favourite tastes of the class it is useful to make a chart or a pictogram. Use graphing software into which the children can put their personal information. Alternatively, create a large pictogram by providing different coloured pieces of paper to represent each of the food tastes. Ask the children to choose the appropriate coloured paper on which to draw their own face and write their name. Suggest they use a facial expression to show how much they like the taste they have chosen. In turn, the children can attach the picture of their face to the prepared chart.

When the pictogram is complete, provide children with their own copies of the computer-generated pictogram or refer them to the large wall chart. Discuss what it shows. Make sure the children are aware that each picture represents one item – in this case one person's taste – and that the longer the column the greater the number it represents. Is it now easy to tell which tastes are popular rather than remembering when people were putting their hands up? Is there a clear favourite? Perhaps two tastes are liked equally? How many more people like a sweet taste than a salty taste? Talk about how the pictogram is easy to understand at a glance. Sentences with the same information would take longer to read and counting children with their hands up does not help when making comparisons. Point out that the pictogram is a permanent record of the children's tastes at this moment.

### Differentiation
Children:
- provide data for a pictogram and talk about the information it shows
- understand how data can be collected and presented; answer questions using information shown on a pictogram
- understand that a pictogram is a method of presenting information and can be used to make comparisons.

**Tasting and eating foods**

## Plenary
Go over the sequence of this activity: the children were involved in a test to decide which tastes they prefer, the information gathered was presented as a pictogram that was used to answer questions and make comparisons. If the pictogram was generated by computer, compare it with any manual pictograms the children have created at other times.

## Display
Add the work from this activity to the food display. Position labelled pictures of different foods under the headings *salty*, *sweet*, *sour* and so on. Perhaps encourage the children to add new information when they have tasted foods at home.

# ACTIVITY 2

# MEALS, SNACKS AND TREATS

SCIENCE

### Learning objective
To recognise a sensible eating pattern.

### Resources
Images to represent meals, snacks and treats, including food packaging; paper, pencils; board or flip chart.

### Preparation
Write out a vocabulary list of food items commonly eaten as snacks and treats. Be aware of the need for sensitivity towards children who may not often have snacks or treats.

### Activity
Begin by asking the children to name the meals they have. List these, indicating in which part of the day these meals usually occur. Breakfast is usually the first meal of the day and is taken after many hours without food, hence its name. Lunch can mean a meal in the middle of the day, as can dinner, especially if taken at school. Do some children have a tea at the end of the afternoon? Perhaps they have tea at weekends but not on school days. Do many children have their dinner in the evening? Perhaps they have supper? Are there any special meals the children can talk about that take place in their families, perhaps to celebrate a religious or family event?

   Decide what a meal is – when different foods and drinks are specially prepared and perhaps eaten as a sequence of different courses. Talk about people going out together for a meal or meeting for a special family meal. Point out that several different foods are eaten during a meal and that this is good practice for maintaining a healthy body.

   Next, talk about snacks. What do the children enjoy as a snack? When do they eat snacks? Are the children able to save their snacks to eat at certain times, probably when they feel hungry? Talk about eating between meals and how too many snacks can stop people feeling hungry and put them off their proper meals, especially if the snacks consist of high-fat or sugary foods, such as sweets, chocolates, crisps and biscuits. Emphasise that eating too much of this type of food is not good for their health and growth. Talk positively about eating snacks of fruit or vegetables, such as carrot sticks, emphasising the importance of fruit and vegetables in their daily diet.

   Remind the children of some of the things they do each day and how they need a variety of foods for their bodies to be able to perform physical and mental activities. (See section 1, activity 1.) Talk about the importance of drinking plenty of water throughout the day. Perhaps some children prefer fizzy drinks instead. Take this opportunity to point out that

**2**

Tasting and eating foods

too many sweet drinks can be detrimental to teeth as well as adding to the children's consumption of sugar.

Ask the children if there are any foods they have occasionally as special treats. They might mention food at birthdays and Christmas – perhaps a special cake, ice cream, chocolate or sweets at weekends if they have been good! Point out that these foods are not usually eaten every day; eating such foods frequently is not good for a healthy body, but they are enjoyable as occasional treats.

## Recording
Ask the children to record the foods they like to eat at different times of the day, including meals and snacks. Ask them to also record what their favourite treat is. Provide sentence starters if necessary: *My favourite meal of the day is ___. The food I like for a snack is ___. For a treat I like ___.* Encourage them to give reasons for their choices where appropriate.

## Differentiation
Children:
- recognise that there is a pattern of meals, that anything eaten between meals is a snack, and treats are eaten occasionally; record simply their own choices
- recognise that there is a pattern of meals, that meals provide a variety of foods, that snacks are eaten between meals and treats occasionally; record their own choices in sentences
- recognise that there is a pattern of meals; understand the importance of meals in providing a variety of foods, that snacks are eaten between meals and treats occasionally; record their choices in detailed explanatory sentences.

## Plenary
Remind the children that eating a variety of foods at meal times is important to good health and that although enjoyable, unhealthy snacks should be limited. Point out that if eaten very often, a food no longer becomes a treat.

## Display
Together, write out a list of meals and definitions of snacks and treats to add to the food display.

## ACTIVITY 3

# PLANNING A MEAL

SCIENCE

## Learning objective
To understand that eating a variety of different foods is important for good health and growth.

## Resources
Pictures showing different foods; wrappers and containers to represent some foods; food-group circles (see Preparation); paper; pencils and crayons.

CURRICULUM LINKS ages 5–7: Food and healthy eating

**Tasting and eating foods**

## Preparation

Write out a menu for a simple meal.

On large sheets of paper, draw circles to represent the five different food groups: two large circles, two half size and one quarter size. Cut pictures from magazines and other publicity materials, and use wrappers and packets to represent foods. Attach these inside the circles: in one large circle, show fruits and vegetables, and in the other a range of bread products, potatoes, pasta and rice. Use one half-size circle to show milk and other dairy products, and the other to show meat and fish. In the small circle show foods containing large amounts of fat or sugar, such as chips, crisps, cakes, biscuits and fizzy drinks.

## Activity

Show the children the circles you have prepared representing the main food groups. Explain that the largest circles show foods we need the most to keep our bodies in good condition and that these should provide the biggest part of our diet (*Eat plenty*). Identify the foods and briefly make connections within the groups: *In this circle there are different types of bread and different types of rice. This circle shows fruits and vegetables, which are similar types of food.* Then explain that the foods in the middle-sized circles are foods we need a moderate amount of (*Eat some*), and those in the small circle are foods we should only eat in smaller quantities (*Eat small amounts*).

Next, describe a meal you have enjoyed and show the children the menu you have written out – perhaps fish and chips, and apple pie with custard. Suggest the children look at the food you have described and decide whether it is considered a balanced meal.

Explain or remind the children that a balanced meal should have a range of foods from different groups, with more foods from the large circles than the other circles. Do the dishes on the menu cover the range of groups? Are there enough foods from the larger circles? Prompt the children to talk about a lack of vegetables. Should you have you included more fruit? Was the portion of chips large or small? Discuss the fact that although chips are made from potatoes they are cooked in fat which puts them in the *Eat small amounts* category. Consider, too, the fat and sugar content of apple pie. Would eating some salad have made the meal more balanced? Perhaps explain that you ate fruit as snacks during the day, which would help to improve the balance.

Revise the menu, perhaps including a starter of some salad or vegetables with the fish and chips and a piece of fruit or fruit salad as dessert. Try to show that having eaten chips, snacks of similar products between meals, such as crisps, would not be a good idea. Enjoying some different fruit would be ideal.

Organise the children into pairs and ask them to work together to devise a menu for a balanced two-course meal. Encourage them to refer to the food groups and include a range of foods in their meal. Ask them also to decide on a suitable snack they would eat at another time during the day.

## Recording

Provide a worksheet on which two plates have been represented. Ask the children to draw and label the foods for their two-course meal, which they have discussed with a partner. By the side of the plates, ask them to draw a snack they might have during the day and a treat they might eat occasionally.

## Differentiation

Children:
- are aware that a variety of foods should be eaten; with help plan a menu for a balanced meal
- plan a simple menu, recognising that a variety of foods is required for a balanced meal
- understand that there are different food groups and that a wide variety of foods is needed for a balanced diet.

Tasting and eating foods

## Plenary
Acknowledge that it can be difficult to decide on a suitable menu and that often the foods we like to eat are in just one or two of the food groups. Point out, however, that a wide variety of foods is important for bodies to remain healthy, particularly children's, which are growing and developing. Explain that for a balanced diet, food choices can stretch over one or two days, and that including a range of foods also makes our diets more interesting.

## Display
Develop the food display by arranging the circles, appropriately labelled, and perhaps including the children's menus. Alternatively, present the menus in a folder with symbols indicating special healthy eating awards.

### ACTIVITY 4

# THE IMPORTANCE OF FRUITS AND VEGETABLES

SCIENCE

## Learning objective
To know that fruits and vegetables have nutritional value and are an important part of our diet.

## Resources
A picnic basket or lunch box; snack food items to include: fruit, such as an apple, a banana, and a handful of dried fruit, a packet of crisps and other similar processed food, a chocolate biscuit; coloured paper/stickers for tickets; small 'post box'; large sheet of paper for a graph; graphing computer software; paper, pencils and crayons.

## Preparation
Make arrangements for another class to take part in the choice test and later receive the results. Plan the method of producing the graph, whether manually or using computer software.

## Activity
Present the food items in a basket or lunch box and identify them with the children. Point out that they are foods regarded as snacks and would be eaten between meals if someone was feeling hungry and needed a small amount of food. Ask the children to decide which item they would have if given a choice. Perhaps use a show of hands to assess the popularity of each snack. Make some generalisations: *Most people would choose the packet of crisps/ apple. Only a few people would choose the banana/chocolate biscuit. No one has picked the dried fruit/crisps as their first choice.*

**Tasting and eating foods**

Remind the children of the previous activity and ask them to consider which types of food they should eat the most of. Consider which snack foods would help the most with providing a healthy diet and therefore should be eaten most often. Explain that fruits, together with vegetables, are important foods because they help to make our bodies strong and healthy.

Point out that many of the foods produced especially for snacks are not the best foods for our bodies, even though we enjoy them. Suggest that eating fruits more often than processed snacks is much better for children's bodies to grow strong and healthy. Stress the need for balance.

Remind the children that a balanced diet means eating a variety of foods over a period of time, perhaps a few days, and that fruit and vegetables should be an important part of meal times.

Point out that athletes and other sports people will eat large amounts of fruits and vegetables to make sure their bodies perform well. If appropriate, explain that fruits and vegetables contain vitamins and minerals, which are especially good for healthy bodies.

Suggest the children find out which snack foods are preferred by children in another class. They could prepare a simple test that involves asking other children to decide between snacks (ideally those that have been discussed). Arrange the foods on a table with different coloured 'tickets' next to each one. Explain to the children in the trial that you want to find out which snack they prefer. Ask each of them to take a ticket representing the snack of their choice and post it in a box. Let them know that they will find out the results later.

Ask the children in your class to count the tickets and use the data to produce a wall-mounted, individual or computer-generated graph (for example, a pictogram or bar chart). Discuss the information the graph shows. Which is the favourite snack? Is there a snack no one has chosen? What does the graph tell us about the eating preferences of the children in the other class? Encourage the children's comments in the light of the knowledge they have about a balanced diet. Are these children eating healthily? Perhaps they enjoy fruit rather than prepared snacks. If not, do they need any advice? Perhaps if they eat lots of fruit and vegetables at meal times they will have a balanced diet.

### Recording
In the light of the information collected, ask the children to write a conclusion for the other class, congratulating or advising them on their choices of snacks.

### Differentiation
Children:
■ know that it is important to eat lots of fruits and vegetables
■ understand that fruits and vegetables are important as part of a balanced diet
■ understand that fruits and vegetables have nutritional value and are an important part of a balanced diet.

### Display
Add a statement to the display focusing on fruit and vegetables, perhaps as a banner proclaiming their importance: *Eat plenty!*

## ACTIVITY 5

## FRUITS AND VEGETABLES – TASTING

DESIGN & TECHNOLOGY

### Learning objectives
To recognise that fruits and vegetables need some preparation before being eaten; to understand that they have different tastes and textures.

## Resources
A selection of fruits and vegetables that can be eaten raw, including some that require peeling, others that just need washing; vegetable peeler; paper plates; kitchen paper; pictures of other fruits that are perhaps unavailable at this time of the year; photocopiable page 29; pencils and crayons.

## Preparation
Have some of each of the fruits and vegetables already prepared – washed, peeled if necessary, and sliced into small pieces. Write in the names of the foods to be tasted on the photocopiable sheet. Ask the children to wash their hands immediately before the activity.

## Activity
Explain to the children that they will have the opportunity to taste some fruits and vegetables during the activity, which is why they have been asked to wash their hands.

Show the children the selection of fruits and vegetables you have assembled and comment on how tempting and fresh they look. Ask the children if they think it is wise to eat fruits and vegetables. Refer to activities 3 and 4 and remind the children that fruits and vegetables form one of the two most important groups of food we should eat.

Identify the fruits and vegetables and point out that they can be eaten raw. Explain that although these foods can be eaten as they are, they require some minimal preparation. Choose one of the fruits, for example a banana, and ask the children what they would need to do with this fruit before eating it. As you demonstrate peeling the banana, point out how the skin keeps the fruit inside fresh and clean. Ask which other fruits they can see that have skin or peel that needs removing before the fruit can be eaten. Group these together. Peel a satsuma or other citrus fruit, then show how the skin of a carrot needs to be removed with a peeler. Ask the children to name other fruits and vegetables that have peel or skin that needs removing before the food is eaten (pineapple, melon, potato, onion, and so on). Refer to pictures where these fruits and vegetables are not available.

Consider which fruits and vegetables can be eaten without peeling and discuss why they need washing – people have handled them, there may be dust and germs on them, chemicals may have been sprayed on them. Examine and talk about apples, grapes, plums, also lettuce and cabbage. Show pictures of other fruits and vegetables the children might mention.

## Recording
Tell the children you have prepared small samples of fruits and vegetables which they can taste, and then record some information about their textures. Ask them to decide whether each sample they taste is crunchy, soft, juicy or chewy. Show the children photocopiable page 29 and explain how they can record the information using ticks after each tasting. Point out that some foods might have more than one quality, for example a fruit might be both soft and juicy. After tasting all the samples, ask the children to comment on their tasting experiences in the space provided at the bottom of the page: *The fruit I liked best was the orange because it was soft and juicy.*

© Nova Developments

## Differentiation
Children:
■ recognise some differences between fruits and vegetables that can be eaten raw; record their tasting experiences in a chart

**Tasting and eating foods**

■ know that fruits and vegetables can be eaten raw with minimal preparation; record their tasting experiences in a chart and with sentences
■ understand the minimal preparation needed before eating different raw fruits and vegetables, recording information as a chart and in writing.

### Plenary
Discuss how enjoyable the tasting tests were. Ask the children to refer to their charts and find out which of the samples they found to be juicy. Do they all agree? Talk about which fruits and vegetables were soft and which were found to be crunchy. Remind the children that fruit and vegetables with an edible skin need to be washed before eating.

### Display
Include the charts in the fruits and vegetables display.

## ACTIVITY 6

# FRUITS AND VEGETABLES – PREPARING

DESIGN & TECHNOLOGY

### Learning objectives
To use hand tools and practise simple food-processing skills; to understand the importance of working in a hygienic manner.

### Resources
Fruit bowl or basket; fruits and vegetables that can easily be handled by the children, for example bananas and satsumas for peeling, oranges for squeezing, carrots for grating, and bananas, apples and cabbage for slicing; simple safe tools such as a plastic fruit squeezer, plastic grater/shredder, peelers, serrated knives without pointed ends, small forks and so on; chopping boards; paper plates; plastic jugs; kitchen paper; antibacterial wipes; plastic table covering; paper, pencils and crayons.

### Preparation
Arrange the fruits and vegetables in a bowl or basket. Prepare a work surface where different processes can be demonstrated in front of the children.
  Decide how the children's practical activities will be organised. Depending on space and availability of helpers, the children can work simultaneously or one group at a time. Alternatively, a group can practise a different process each day so that all the children can eat the foods over a period of time.
  Assess and minimise the risk of using knives and other equipment with sharp edges.

### Activity
Show the children the selection of fruits and vegetables. Comment on their attractive appearance, how colourful, fresh and tempting they look and how good they are to eat, as well as providing important nourishment for our bodies.
  Explain to the children that there are ways to prepare fruit and vegetables even when they are to be eaten raw. Ask if they can offer any suggestions. From the previous activity, they should be able to tell you that some fruits and vegetables need peeling and others need to be washed before they are eaten. Identify fruits and vegetables among the selection that require these treatments. Tell the children that you have washed your hands thoroughly as you will be handling the fruit that will be eaten later.
  Ask the children how a banana or apple can be shared. What is needed if these fruits are to be divided? Show the children a knife and demonstrate how it can be used safely and

## Tasting and eating foods

efficiently to cut a banana, an apple and a cabbage. Point out how easy it is to slice a banana into circles as the flesh of the fruit is quite soft. Show the children how to slice half an apple with its cut side on the chopping board and holding it firmly with one hand or a fork. Point out the danger of cutting fingers if the slicing is not done very carefully. Similarly, slice half a cabbage, explaining that small pieces of this raw vegetable are tasty and extremely good for keeping the body healthy. Carefully arrange the sliced foods on plates.

Next, show the children the citrus squeezer and see if any of them can describe its use. Demonstrate how the juice of an orange can be obtained by using this simple piece of equipment. Pour the juice into a jug for use later. Ask which other fruits are really juicy and could be squeezed to provide a drink. Explain that some fruits need special equipment to extract the juice as they are not easy to squeeze by hand.

Finally produce the grater/shredder. Ask if anyone has used such a piece of equipment before and demonstrate shredding a carrot. Point out the hazard of damaging fingers on the sharp parts of the equipment and give advice on safe handling. Can the children suggest other fruits and vegetables that could be shredded? Try shredding some apple and cabbage. Do they think a banana could be prepared in this way? Ask the children why they think it is useful to shred or grate fruits and vegetables.

Tell the children they will have the opportunity to try these different treatments and explain the procedure you have planned. Insist that hands are thoroughly washed before any preparation takes place, that the children know the tools, equipment and working surfaces are perfectly clean, that the fruit has been washed as appropriate, and that they are aware of the risks of using the tools.

Under careful supervision, let the children explore these preparation methods.

## Recording
Suggest the children examine, draw and label some of the tools used to prepare the foods and list the names of fruits and vegetables that can be treated in this way. Encourage them to include instructions for using the individual tools safely. They can compile a code of practice to include washing hands, preparing a suitable work surface, checking equipment is clean, handling tools safely, cleaning and tidying up afterwards.

## Differentiation
Children:
■ practise simple methods of preparing fruits and vegetables, recognising the need for cleanliness and safe handling of tools
■ practise different methods of preparing fruits and vegetables, working in a hygienic manner and handling tools safely
■ practise different methods of preparing fruit and vegetables, understanding the importance of working in a hygienic manner and using tools safely and efficiently.

## Plenary
Talk about the children's efforts at slicing, chopping, squeezing, shredding and so on, and how useful these skills will be when preparing fruits and vegetables in the future. Remind the children how cleanliness and safety play an important part in eating healthily.

## Display
Label and display safe tools with simple instructions for their use. Include a vocabulary list of the verbs relating to food preparation.

**2**

Tasting and eating foods

## ACTIVITY 7

## FRUITS AND VEGETABLES – PROCESSING

DESIGN & TECHNOLOGY

### Learning objective
To recognise that processing food can affect appearance, texture, odour and colour.

### Resources
Examples of a fruit and a vegetable to taste before and after cooking (apples are ideal fruits for eating raw and when cooked; carrots and cabbage are enjoyed raw as well as after cooking); dishes, spoons and kitchen paper; photocopiable page 30; board or flip chart.

### Preparation
Cook each type of fruit and vegetable selected for the activity.

### Activity
Talk about the enjoyment of eating fresh fruit and how important it is in our diet. Comment on vegetables the children have eaten raw. Point out that some vegetables are usually cooked before we eat them. Ask the children if they can think of any cooked vegetables they eat. Make a list and tick any that can be enjoyed raw as well. Move on to discuss cooked fruit and list any the children have enjoyed which have been cooked, perhaps in pies and puddings.

  Show the children a fruit before and after preparation and cooking. This could be sliced raw apple and stewed apple. Explain that cooking involves heating, which causes changes to take place. Ask the children to look carefully at the 'before' and 'after' samples. Prompt them to notice changes in appearance, including colour, and observable differences in texture. Encourage words such as *firm* and *soft*, *light* and *dark*, *shiny* and *dull*. Discuss handling cooked apple compared with a raw apple; how tools are needed when food is cooked as it loses its shape and is less easy to handle, and the juice begins to run out. It may also be hot.

  Now show examples of a raw and cooked vegetable, perhaps cabbage or carrot. As before, compare appearance, colour and observable texture of the raw and cooked food.

  Let the children experience the differences in smell and taste between the raw and the cooked foods. Emphasise the importance of this test, encouraging the children to take it seriously and record their observations after each tasting.

### Recording
The children can use photocopiable page 30 to record their observations and experiences of the fruit and the vegetable when raw and when cooked. Show them where to write in the name, and perhaps illustrate the examples of the fruit and the vegetable used.

### Differentiation
Children:
■ recognise and record some differences between raw and cooked fruits and vegetables
■ are aware of and record changes that take place when fruits and vegetables are cooked
■ understand that changes take place when fruits and vegetables are cooked, recording details of observations.

### Plenary
Recap on some of the changes which take place when specific fruits and vegetables are cooked. Comment on changes in taste and texture and how this gives us different ways of enjoying fruits and vegetables as an important part of our everyday eating patterns.

### Display
Make a vocabulary list of adjectives used to compare raw and cooked fruits and vegetables.

Tasting and eating foods

# Tasting fruits and vegetables

| name of food | crunchy | soft | juicy | chewy |
|---|---|---|---|---|
|  |  |  |  |  |

The fruit I liked best was _____

_____

_____

The vegetable I liked best was _____

_____

_____

CURRICULUM LINKS ages 5–7: Food and healthy eating

# Raw and cooked

|  | appearance | smell | taste |
|---|---|---|---|
| raw fruit | | | |
| cooked fruit | | | |
| raw vegetable | | | |
| cooked vegetable | | | |

Tasting and eating foods

CURRICULUM LINKS ages 5–7: Food and healthy eating

# Eat more fruit and vegetables

## Section 3

**FOCUS**
DESIGN & TECHNOLOGY
- Investigating the range of foods made from fruits and vegetables
- Planning and creating a special product using fruits/vegetables
- Considering efficient working practices
- Hygiene and safety issues
- Evaluating the product

## Preparation for section 3

If possible, arrange a designated 'kitchen' space to include storage and working areas. Make labels to show where tools and equipment will be kept so the children can locate and return items they need. Point out instructions to remind the children about efficient working practices, and hygiene and safety issues. Provide sufficient table coverings, cleaning equipment and waste bins if large numbers of children are working at the same time.

## ACTIVITY 1

### CREATING A SPECIAL PRODUCT

DESIGN & TECHNOLOGY

### Learning objectives
To understand there are many ways of eating fruits and vegetables; to consider ways of encouraging others to eat more fruit and vegetables.

### Resources
Paper, pencils and crayons; board or flip chart.

### Activity
Talk about how good some fruits and vegetables are as snacks. They only need minimal preparation, and we need to eat lots of them to keep us healthy. Point out that fruits and vegetables can also be used to make more complex dishes. Ask the children to think of as many foods as possible that are made with fruits and vegetables. List these on the board under separate *Fruit* and *Vegetables* headings, for example salads, jelly, stir-fries, soup, curry, yogurt, fruit drinks.

Encourage the children to talk about when and where they have tried these dishes. Did they help prepare them? Which are their favourites? Distinguish between dishes which use raw fruits and vegetables and those in which the foods are cooked. Ask the children to tell you about some of the methods used when cooking fruits and vegetables at home.

Now focus on a point that has arisen in a previous activity relating to the amount of fruits and vegetables people eat. Results of the survey in section 2, activity 4 might show that the opportunity to eat fruit is not always taken – that children tend to prefer a different type of snack food. Perhaps the children in your class have realised that they do not eat enough fruit

**3**

Eat more fruit and vegetables

and vegetables. Ask what they could do to encourage others to eat more of these foods. Suggest that as well as trying to persuade people through discussion, it would be a good idea to provide samples of fruits and vegetables for them to taste. People who do not eat many fruits and vegetables might not realise the many ways of eating them, or they could be reluctant to try different foods. Suggest providing products which would tempt these reluctant fruit-and-vegetable eaters and help them to follow a healthy eating pattern. Guide the children towards the idea of creating a special 'dish of the day' for others to try.

Look at the list of foods containing fruits and vegetables. Decide which would be ideal for persuading others to enjoy more fruits and vegetables. As the food will be prepared in the classroom, briefly explain what facilities are available and whether any cooking is possible. Point out that eating raw fruits and vegetables is a healthy and tasty option.

Ask the children to talk in pairs about using fruits and vegetables to create a special dish. Tell them who they will be designing the dish for. Encourage them to think about making the food look attractive by using different shapes, colours and textures in their design, as well as considering scent and taste. Refer to the children's experiences of experimenting with fruit and vegetables in previous activities.

### Recording
Ask the children to write a description of the fruit and vegetable dish they think would encourage others to eat more of these foods. They can draw and label their impression of the finished product, and suggest at what time of day it should be eaten.

### Differentiation
Children:
- know of many ways of eating fruits and vegetables; provide ideas for creating a product to encourage others to eat more fruit and vegetables, recording it with a labelled drawing
- know of many ways of eating fruits and vegetables; are aware that some people need encouragement to eat more fruit and vegetables; contribute ideas towards designing a product and record this using notes and a drawing
- know of many ways of eating fruits and vegetables; provide ideas in discussion to encourage people to eat more fruit and vegetables, recording design ideas for a special product with detailed notes and a drawing.

### Plenary
Pick out some of the children's suggestions for creating a fruit and vegetable dish. Praise ideas where thought has been given to the design in terms of colour, shape, texture, scent and taste. Perhaps use some of the ideas for the whole class to use in their design project.

### Display
Arrange all of the children's design ideas so that they can be admired and discussed.

## ACTIVITY 2

## PLANNING THE PRODUCT

DESIGN & TECHNOLOGY

### Learning objective
To develop a plan and communicate what they intend to make.

### Resources
The developing fruits and vegetables display; the children's ideas from the previous activity; paper, pencils and crayons.

## Preparation

Decide on the organisation of the designing and making task. Assess the time and help available and the resources required, and consider whether the whole class will be involved in making the same product. Choose what the product will be, for example a fruit salad, and try to consciously incorporate some of the children's ideas from the previous activity. Alternatively, groups of children can create different products, some using fruit and others using vegetables.

On a large sheet of paper, prepare a framework for the plan. This might include questions to be addressed, for example:

- The aim of the activity – what are we trying to do?
- The product – what will we make?
- The target group – who is our product for?
- The ingredients and quantities – what fruits/vegetables will we need? How much of each type of fruit/vegetable is required?
- Processes involved – how will we prepare the fruits/vegetables?
- Tools and equipment – what will we need?
- Procedure – in what order will we do things? How will we present the finished product?
- Time – how long do we think it will take us to complete the task?

(Hygiene and safety issues are dealt with in Activity 3.)

Eat more fruit and vegetables

## Activity

Tell the children that they will be using the knowledge they have gained, and the skills they have learned, to design and make a fruit or vegetables product that will encourage others to enjoy eating more of this type of food. Refer to the previous activity, where the children produced ideas for a special dish, and explain how some of those suggestions can be used in this project.

Establish who will try out the food – the target group – and guide the children towards considering the product you intend them to create. Discuss which aspects of the children's designs can be used and should appeal to the target group. Build up a picture of the product. Talk about the ingredients and how they might be prepared. Remind the children of their investigations into the differences among fruits or vegetables (section 1), so they can suggest examples that show contrasting colours, shapes and textures. Refer to the display and the children's previous work.

Emphasise the need for a plan, so that everyone knows what they will be doing and all the things needed will be in place. Show the children the framework you have prepared. Work through each of the questions in turn and develop the plan with the class. Write in the children's suggestions, helping them to address the questions and communicate the important information briefly and to the point. Make sure that the children are aware of the order in which the tasks are to be carried out.

Encourage the children to think of a special name for the product, perhaps relating to the ingredients and the people involved in its design.

## Recording

For each child, print out a copy of the questions and answers on the plan. Ask each child to make their own illustration of how the product will look, taking into account the decisions made by the class. Suggest that the children write a heading, labels and a sentence that describes the product attractively.

## Differentiation

Children:
- suggest some ideas when planning a product, communicating what they intend to make with a simple labelled drawing

Eat more fruit and vegetables

■ suggest ideas for a product, conscious of the need for making a plan; communicate what they intend to make with a detailed labelled drawing
■ suggest relevant and imaginative ideas for a product, understanding the need for a plan; communicate what they intend to make with an appropriately labelled drawing.

## Plenary
Congratulate the children on their planning skills. Explain that the plan has helped to address problems: by consulting the plan, everything will be in place and everyone has a clear idea of what is to be done and why. Admire the illustrations the children have done of the finished product.

## Display
Display the plan and the children's illustrations.

# ACTIVITY 3

# HYGIENE AND SAFETY

DESIGN & TECHNOLOGY

## Learning objective
To recognise hygienic practices when handling food and know how to control risk by following simple instructions.

## Resources
Photocopiable page 39; board or flip chart; paper, pencils and crayons; the 'kitchen' work area and equipment.

## Activity
Organise the children into pairs, providing each pair with photocopiable page 39, which shows two children working inefficiently in chaotic conditions while preparing food. Ask the children to look carefully at the illustration and point out to each other what the children in

CURRICULUM LINKS ages 5–7: Food and healthy eating

the picture are doing wrong. Encourage them to consider how things could be improved.

After about five minutes, bring the class together and discuss the children's ideas. Begin to compile a list of the suggestions in the form of notes. Arrange these into groups, such as *working tidily, working safely, working cleanly/hygienically*.

Referring to the photocopiable page, discuss how spillage and clutter might be avoided. Talk about working efficiently, moving about carefully, and arranging items to be used tidily and away from the edges of surfaces. Remind the children about clearing everything away after they have finished.

Talk about using equipment and tools safely. Can the children remind each other of how to use a knife safely from previous experience? (See section 2, activity 6.) How do we avoid accidents when using a grater or peeler?

Emphasise hygienic practices. First talk about personal cleanliness, such as the importance of washing hands thoroughly before handling food, keeping long hair out of the way and not licking fingers. Discuss making sure tools, equipment and surfaces are also thoroughly clean. Explain how wearing a clean apron not only protects clothes but helps to keep germs away from food.

Suggest there are many children like the two in the picture, who would benefit from some instructions to help them work more efficiently and safely. Ask the children to think of some simple instructions to form a code, to use when preparing food. The children can work in pairs again to try out ideas, or work together as a class.

Discuss the ideas and draw up a class code of instructions to be followed. For example:
- Wash hands thoroughly before handling food.
- Keep work surfaces clean and tidy.
- Organise your ingredients and equipment.
- Take care with sharp tools.
- Move about carefully to avoid spilling and knocking things over.

If appropriate at this point, introduce the children to the working area, so they can become familiar with the layout of the tools and equipment, understand the procedures for washing hands and cleaning surfaces, and so on.

## Recording
Ask the children to write out and illustrate their own or the class code.

## Plenary
Point out how useful instructions are when making anything, so that a task can be performed safely and efficiently and, when working with food, in a hygienic manner.

## Display
Display a copy of the code in the working area.

## ACTIVITY 4

# MAKING THE PRODUCT

DESIGN & TECHNOLOGY

## Learning objective
To select and use appropriate fruits and vegetables, processes and tools when making a product.

## Resources
Fruits and vegetables needed to create the product; equipment such as plastic bowls, dishes, graters, juicers, chopping boards, suitable knives and peelers, and spoons; aprons;

**Eat more fruit and vegetables**

plastic cloth to cover working surfaces; kitchen roll; cleaning cloths and antibacterial wipes; containers for waste material; camera; paper, pencils and crayons.

## Preparation

Plan the procedure of the activity in detail. Decide whether all the children will work at the same time or in groups. Ideally, arrange the work area so that it can be kept tidy, and tools and equipment are labelled and easily accessible. Allocate tasks to individuals so that everyone has the opportunity to play an important part in making the product. Arrange the fruits and vegetables in baskets or bowls. Allow sufficient ingredients so that the children, as well as the intended target group, can sample the product, and make arrangements for this sampling. Have a sink or bowls of water ready in which the children can rinse food as appropriate. Assess and minimise the risks encountered when using knives and other equipment with sharp edges.

Beforehand, tell the children when they will be preparing their product and whether they need to bring their own apron. Briefly explain the procedure so that they know at which point they will be involved.

Arrange to take photographs of the children at work, as well as of the finished products.

If other children are to be involved in sampling the product, arrange a way of communicating their reactions to the class. Perhaps the members of the target group could write a simple comment or answer specific questions about their experience. For example, *Have you tried this food before? What did you enjoy about the product? Would you like to eat this food again?*

## Activity

Remind the children that they have practised using tools and equipment, and understand that following instructions is important. They also know that working in a hygienic manner is important. In addition, they have designed and planned a product to make for a particular purpose. With all this experience and newly learned skills, the children are now ready to create the product.

Refer the children to the plan and specific additions to the code of practice. For example, tell each group that they are responsible for checking:

- hands are well washed
- fruits/vegetables are selected as planned
- processes are carried out safely

- children work sensibly and efficiently
- hygienic conditions are maintained
- waste is disposed of as appropriate
- attention is paid to presentation
- children help with the clearing up.

Afterwards, make special arrangements for tasting the product. (If the food is not sampled immediately, cover it up and keep it cool.) Ask the children to consider the presentation of the product, to sniff the scents and eat the food slowly. Encourage them to discuss the sensations with their neighbours.

Eat more fruit and vegetables

## Recording
Ask the children to begin an account of their designing and making project, together with appropriate illustrations. They should describe how they were involved in the making processes, which parts they enjoyed doing, any problems they encountered and how these were overcome.

## Differentiation
Children:
- with help select and use fruits/vegetables and simple processes and tools to help create a product
- select and use fruits/vegetables, processes and tools to create a product, working safely and efficiently
- with confidence and imagination, select and use fruits/vegetables, processes and tools to create a product, working safely and efficiently.

## Plenary
Comment on the children's practical abilities. Talk about how well they worked, how they tackled any difficulties, followed instructions and carried out tasks safely and efficiently.

## Display
Arrange captioned photographs as a reminder of the tasks and success of the activity.

# ACTIVITY 5

# EVALUATION

DESIGN & TECHNOLOGY

## Learning objective
To evaluate the product by asking questions.

## Resources
Photographs and the children's accounts of their assignment from the previous activity, comments from the tasting group.

## Activity
Remind the children why they decided to make this dish using fruits/vegetables. Talk about encouraging people to eat more of these foods and why this is beneficial. Do the children think they provided an enjoyable product? Are they pleased with their efforts? Did the product match their original ideas? If there were changes, were these improvements? Did the product look attractive? Smell delicious? Taste good?

If appropriate, discuss the reactions of the target group. Do the children think they have achieved their aim? Will they make a similar food for themselves at home with their parents'/

**3**

Eat more fruit and vegetables

carers' permission? Are there any changes they might try? Perhaps they could alter the ingredients depending on the season and the produce available. Would they use a different process for preparing the food another time – perhaps slicing a particular fruit instead of shredding or cutting a vegetable into smaller or more even pieces?

### Recording
The children can extend the accounts of their efforts at designing and making by describing the finished product and their own and others' reactions to tasting it. Encourage them to conclude whether they think their product is successful in persuading others, as well as themselves, to eat more fruit and vegetables.

### Differentiation
Children:
■ talk about and describe their designing and making assignment; comment on the finished product
■ discuss their designing and making assignment; ask questions about the finished product and consider whether they have achieved their aim
■ discuss a variety of aspects of their designing and making assignment, asking relevant questions and considering the success of their efforts.

### Plenary
Bring the whole project to an end by congratulating the children on their efforts. Find out if they enjoyed their involvement in creating the product.
  Did they think they would create something they liked? Has the experience changed any ideas they had about eating fruits and vegetables? Will they be eating more of these foods in the future? Are they keen to make the dish (or a similar one) at home?

### Display
Print out some of the children's evaluation comments to complete the display.

Eat more fruit and vegetables

DESIGN & TECHNOLOGY

# Correct the chaos

Hannah and Jay are preparing some fruit and vegetable dishes, but they need help! What advice would you give them?

# Section 4

# Exercise

## FOCUS
### SCIENCE
- achieving good health through exercise
- the importance of exercise for a healthy body
- encouraging regular exercise
- different ways of enjoying exercise

### Preparation for section 4
Consider any children with disabilities or weight problems and adjust these activities accordingly. Encourage sensitivity towards all children, and try to make all the activities inclusive and enjoyable.

Make arrangements for some PE sessions to take place in the hall or outdoors, particularly for activity 3. Take the opportunity of a spare moment during the day to encourage the children to practise simple exercises, as in activity 2.

## ACTIVITY 1

### EXERCISE TO STAY HEALTHY

### Learning objective
To understand that we need exercise to keep healthy.

### Resources
Posters, other images and video clips showing children and adults in sports and active pursuits; photocopiable page 46; pencils and crayons; board or flip chart.

### Preparation
Plan time for the children to fill in their exercise diaries each day for a week, perhaps recording the previous day's activities each morning.

### Activity
Ask the children what exercise is. Talk about moving their bodies in different ways: vigorously, more gently, on their own or with others. What exercise have they done today? Did they walk to school? Were they active in the playground, enjoying running and jumping? Has there been a PE or games lesson? Point out that although our bodies need rest, which we get when we sleep or sit quietly, our bodies also need exercise every day if we are to stay healthy.

List different kinds of exercise the children might do. Include walking, running, cycling, swimming, dance, as well as the sports they like. Explain that exercise does not have to be tough and very energetic, although it is good to get out of breath at least once every day.

Tell the children that all parts of their bodies need exercising each day to keep them in good working order. At school, PE and games lessons are enjoyable and help them to keep fit in this way. However, it is important that our bodies are active on other days too. Ask the children to think of ideas for exercising their bodies themselves, and write them on the board or flip chart. Talk about walking or cycling to school rather than riding in a car, practising ball games instead of watching television for a long period, and dancing to their favourite music. Point out that exercise can be done individually, not just as a sport with a group of people.

Ask the children to think of symbols that could be used to represent different types of exercise. Draw these next to the activities listed. Perhaps use stick men in different positions to show running, walking, swimming and so on, or draw shoes, waves, balls and rackets. Show pictures of people engaged in different activities to prompt ideas. You could also use a video clip to show a range of different activities.

Exercise

### Recording
Show the children photocopiable page 46. Explain that the columns give the days of a week in which they can record the exercise they do each day. As there is only a small space, the children can use symbols to show the activities they have been involved in. As well as exercise they have done already, will they be doing any activities after school that involve exercise? Perhaps they will go swimming, ride a bike, or take part in a game with their siblings? Show the children how to use the key on the photocopiable. There is space for them to include activities specific to themselves.

### Differentiation
Children:
- are aware that they need to exercise each day; with help record daily activities in a chart
- understand the importance of daily exercise; monitor their exercise pattern over a week and record activities in a chart
- understand the importance of daily exercise; competently monitor their exercise pattern over a week and record activities accurately in a chart.

### Plenary
Encourage the children to remember any exercise that they do so they can complete their charts accurately. Remind them how important it is to make sure their bodies are active in some way every day; not just in school PE and games lessons.

After a week, encourage the children to look carefully at their exercise diaries. Perhaps in pairs, they can help each other to assess and improve if necessary their weekly exercise pattern. Are there days when they did very little exercise? If so, what can they do to make sure they are physically active on these days too?

### Display
Begin a display to encourage good exercise habits. Ask the children to suggest headings, and draw or cut out figures for the display's border. Include images of adults and children in active pursuits. Put the children's charts in a suitably labelled folder or box file near by.

## ACTIVITY 2

# SIMPLE EXERCISES

SCIENCE

### Learning objective
To know that simple exercises practised frequently are helpful for keeping our bodies healthy.

### Resources
Pictures of children exercising, with parts of the body labelled; names of body parts on large cards; paper, pencils and crayons.

CURRICULUM LINKS ages 5–7: Food and healthy eating

Exercise

### Preparation
Write or print out parts of the body that need exercising regularly, either as a list or as separate labels that can be used in the display.

### Activity
When the children are sitting in the classroom, ideally on the floor, encourage them to perform some simple exercises. Explain that as space is limited, the movements should be made carefully and slowly. As the children perform these movements, talk about which parts of their bodies are being exercised.

Demonstrate the movements, emphasising slowness and care, as you ask the children to:
- take two deep breaths, slowly and quietly, in a controlled way, to exercise the lungs and heart
- stretch arms towards the ceiling; wriggle the fingers; spread the fingers; clench fists and circle the wrists
- stretch arms upwards again; clasp hands, stretching as much as possible; then slowly lower clasped hands with arms stretched in front
- clasp hands behind the back, leaning back slightly
- with arms folded behind the back, twist to look to each side
- with arms folded in front, turn head and neck only, to look over each shoulder
- with arms folded in front, twist from the waist to look in each direction
- lift each shoulder in turn to rub ear
- circle both shoulders forwards, then backwards
- look downwards, then upwards, only moving the head
- keeping bottom firmly on the floor, lean to one side, then the other
- put hands on shoulders and circle elbows forwards, then backwards
- with knees bent, bend the back and bring head over to touch knees.

To finish, suggest the children gently stretch to pat themselves on the back.

Talk about the range of upper body parts that have been exercised by slow movements and stretches. Some of these parts would not have been exercised when moving about normally. Tell the children that regular, simple exercises can help keep the whole body in good working order, letting us perform all the movements we need to and enjoy. Point out that they will be able to exercise more actively at playtime or during a PE session.

Depending on the space available, you could extend the movements to include the lower body, such as wriggling toes, bending knees and circling ankles. At other times, hold up cards with names of the parts of the body the children should exercise.

### Recording
The children can draw themselves performing these exercises, writing captions to explain which body parts are being exercised. Use the labelled pictures and vocabulary cards.

### Differentiation
Children:
- perform simple exercises sensibly, aware of how they can keep different parts of their bodies fit and healthy
- perform simple exercises sensibly, providing ideas and understanding the importance of keeping different body parts fit and healthy
- perform simple exercises efficiently, providing useful additional ideas and understanding the importance of keeping different body parts fit and healthy.

### Plenary
Praise the children and say that their bodies will become strong and fit with regular exercise.

### Display
Develop the display, exhibiting the labels of body parts in groups, for instance *arms, hands, fingers, wrists, elbows, shoulders*; then *legs, toes, knees*, and so on.

## ACTIVITY 3

### EXERCISE IS FUN

SCIENCE

Exercise

### Learning objective
To know that exercising the whole body regularly is important and enjoyable.

### Resources
PE equipment such as soft balls, quoits, small bats, bean bags, ropes; pencils and crayons.

### Preparation
Depending on the space available, plan a programme of activities that exercises all parts of the body. Use both indoor and outdoor PE sessions to identify parts of the body that are exercised, as well as emphasising the benefits of regular exercise.
  Prepare a recording sheet, perhaps with a centre box for sentences and a large border for illustrations, relating to favourite activities.
  Allow time for the children to change into suitable clothes for PE activities.

### Activity
Begin by asking the children to take three deep breaths to bring fresh/new air into their lungs. Then start with some general warm-up movements.

### Indoors
- Encourage slow stretches of arms, legs and body, gently bending forwards and backwards; exercise legs with the floor supporting the body.
- Make short bursts of vigorous activity: jumping or jogging on the spot then around the room.
- Demonstrate some simple paired activities, using soft balls, bean bags, and so on.
  Towards the end of the session, divide the class in two and ask each half, in turn, to demonstrate ways of exercising parts of their bodies: *Show us how to exercise arms/toes.*

### Outdoors
Encourage activities more suited to outdoor exercise, including running, jumping and twisting, or activities with balls, hoops and skipping ropes. Emphasise how space can be used effectively and safely when exercising the whole body, and how enjoyable outdoor activities can be. Ask the children how they feel. Are they hot, tired, thirsty, out of breath? Do they feel good? Did they enjoy the exercise? How do their various body parts feel?

### Recording
Show the children the prepared sheet and ask them to draw and describe which type of exercise they most enjoy. Do they prefer to do simple exercises, exercises with equipment, games with friends, or the activities they do during organised sessions at school?

### Differentiation
Children:
- are aware that it is important to exercise all parts of the body and that exercise can be fun
- understand that it is important to exercise all parts of the body regularly to keep healthy, and that this can be enjoyable
- understand the importance of regular exercise in maintaining a healthy lifestyle, and that there are enjoyable activities to suit everyone.

### Plenary
Point out to the children that they now know many ways of exercising their bodies. PE and games sessions at school are just some of the ways of helping them to exercise regularly.

Exercise

### Display
Ask the children to help provide slogans/statements to include in the display to express their enjoyment of activities that improve their health.

SCIENCE

## ACTIVITY 4
## BEFORE AND AFTER

### Learning objective
To be aware of differences in the body before and after exercise.

### Resources
Paper, pencils and crayons; board or flip chart.

### Activity
Remind the children of their PE sessions and ask them how they felt after them. Note their comments on the board. They should remember feeling hot, out of breath, tired, ready for a rest, thirsty. They should also have felt well and happy, having enjoyed different activities.

Explain that during the day bodies need different levels of activity. Sometimes they will be resting. At other times they will be moving around, sometimes quite vigorously.

Go on to explain that exercise helps to keep our whole bodies fit and healthy, not just our arms, legs and the other parts we can see, but also the lungs, heart and brain. Regular exercise keeps limbs supple. Practice also means we get better at certain activities, so our skills improve, which makes us feel good and enjoy the activity more fully.

Ask the children how their bodies feel before exercise, which is probably how they feel now, sitting quietly. They should be aware that they are cool, still, rested and breathing normally.

If appropriate, take the children outside for a short spell of vigorous exercise, so they can focus on how their bodies feel compared with sitting still in the classroom.

### Recording
Ask the children to draw themselves resting, and write about how they feel; then do the same for how they feel after exercise. Some children might explain the benefits of exercise.

### Differentiation
Children:
- are aware of changes to their bodies after exercising, recording this with drawings and simple sentences
- recognise changes to their bodies after exercise, describing this with drawings and sentences
- recognise changes to their bodies after exercise, giving a detailed description of this with drawings and sentences; describe some benefits of exercise.

### Plenary
Point out that because our bodies become hot and sweaty we have special clothes for PE. It is pleasant and hygienic to put clean clothes on after exercise.

Explain to the children how much fitter their bodies become after exercise, and that combined with a balanced diet, this will help them to remain healthy.

### Display
Include key words and phrases to describe how the children feel before and after exercise, as well as the children's work.

## ACTIVITY 5

### AN EXERCISE PLAN

SCIENCE

Exercise

### Learning objective
To consider a personal exercise plan.

### Resources
Paper, pencils and crayons; board or flip chart.

### Activity
Tell the children that there are many opportunities for exercising and that it is important to find ways of keeping fit throughout their lives. Point out that not everyone will want to play football, for example, or cycle every day, but as there are many different ways of keeping fit, it is possible for everyone to find something enjoyable. List all the different ways of exercising the children can think of. Include swimming, riding a bike, playing ball games, walking, skipping, gymnastics, dance and school PE activities. Encourage them to think of what their parents/carers and older siblings do as well.

Tell the children they can organise simple exercises that do not need any special equipment. Remind them of the exercises they noted in their diaries in activity 1 and the exercises they do in school. In pairs, ask them to devise a simple sequence of movements that they could demonstrate to others. Ask them to think about which parts of their bodies they want to exercise. For example, they could plan movements to exercise mainly the legs and feet or a sequence to exercise the whole body.

Encourage the children to practise and demonstrate their exercises. Choose particularly good ideas for the rest of the class to copy. Perhaps reserve a little time each day for a different exercise.

### Recording
Ask the children to include their movements/sequences in the compilation of a weekly exercise plan for themselves. Suggest they consider their plan in three parts: exercise they do at school; exercise they do out of school, perhaps with parents/carers or older siblings; and simple movements they can do by themselves more or less anywhere.

### Differentiation
Children:
■ are aware they need regular exercise to remain fit and healthy; make a simple plan of activities
■ know that there are many ways of exercising to remain fit and healthy; organise a simple plan of suitable activities
■ understand the importance of exercising to remain fit and healthy; plan a range of activities in which they are, or could be, involved.

© Nova Developments

### Plenary
Comment on how fit and healthy the children will be if they exercise regularly. Point out that by combining exercise with sensible eating, the children will feel good, enjoy themselves and grow into strong, healthy adults.

### Display
Complete the display by asking the children to help you find stories, poems, photographs and illustrations relating to exercise, well-being and healthy living.

CURRICULUM LINKS ages 5–7: Food and healthy eating

Exercise

# My exercise diary

| Monday | Tuesday | Wednesday | Thursday | Friday | Saturday | Sunday |
|---|---|---|---|---|---|---|
|  |  |  |  |  |  |  |

| walking | cycling |
|---|---|
| swimming | PE lesson |

CURRICULUM LINKS ages 5–7: Food and healthy eating

# Medicines

Section 5

SCIENCE

## FOCUS
**SCIENCE**
- health and illness
- taking medicines
- asking questions about health and medicines
- communicating information about using medicines safely

SCIENCE

### ACTIVITY 1

### WHEN WE ARE ILL

### Learning objective
To understand that sometimes we become ill and need to take medicines to help us get better.

### Resources
Doll, model or picture to represent a sick child; books, leaflets and posters relating to child health issues; paper, pencils and crayons.

### Preparation
Consider any individuals with serious or on-going health problems and conduct the discussion of the activity with sensitivity. Prepare a vocabulary list to include words such as *well, ill, sick, pain, ache, sore, nurse, doctor, appointment, visit, patient*, and so on.

### Activity
Explain to the children that in spite of eating healthily and taking regular exercise, people do become ill from time to time. They catch colds, get stomach bugs and have things go wrong with different parts of their bodies.

Use the doll, model or picture, or a child taking on the role of a sick child, to help create a scenario that shows what might happen when a person becomes ill. Suggest that the child has a sore throat or a rash and feels unwell. What might be the sequence of events that follows? What do the children do first of all when they feel ill? They will suggest telling their mum or dad or carer about how they feel. Encourage the children to give advice to the patient. They might suggest he or she rests, keeps warm, has a lie down, goes to sleep for a while or has a warm drink. Some might mention special remedies their families use and medicines they have tried before and know will work safely. This might be a linctus

CURRICULUM LINKS ages 5–7: Food and healthy eating

## Medicines

for a sore throat or a cream to put on a rash. Explain that children must always listen to their parents'/carers' instructions and not try anything like this for themselves.

If the patient does not get better soon, what should the next step be? The children might suggest a visit to the nurse or doctor. Point out that nurses and doctors have more experience in dealing with people who are unwell and can therefore recommend special medicines when they have examined a patient.

Medicines are drugs specially made to help sick people. They can be in the form of tablets to be swallowed, liquids to drink, drops for eyes or ears, cream to rub on parts of the body and sometimes injections to put the medicine in the body where it is needed. Following the advice and care from a doctor or nurse and taking special medicines should mean the patient recovers quickly. Emphasise again that parents/carers should be in control of any medicines. Use pictures and other informative material to illustrate points in the discussion.

Ask the children to raise their hands if they have ever needed to visit a doctor or a nurse. Encourage some individuals to share their experiences of visiting the doctor. Point out that sometimes visits are made to avoid children getting ill, especially when having vaccinations to prevent certain diseases. At other times it is necessary to go to hospital to be seen by the doctors there and perhaps stay overnight. Explain that some people need medicines all the time to keep them well.

### Recording

Ask the children to use sentences and illustrations to record a visit they have made to a doctor or nurse. Encourage them to explain how they felt when they were ill, how the medical practitioner helped them, and to mention any medicines they needed to make them well again. Suggest some children describe their experiences of when a sibling was ill, if this is more appropriate.

### Differentiation

Children:
- know that sometimes they will get ill and that it might be necessary to visit a doctor and take medicines, recording personal experiences with illustrations and simple sentences
- understand that when they are ill it might be necessary to visit a doctor and take medicines, recording personal experiences with sentences and illustrations
- understand that when they become ill it might be necessary to visit a doctor and take medicines, recording personal experiences with detailed sentences and illustrations.

### Plenary

Ask some children to read out their sentences, relating personal experiences of being ill. Observe that we are all ill at times and sometimes need the care and skills of a nurse or doctor to help us become well again. Refer the children to any relevant classroom books they might like to read.

### Display

Arrange a corner of the classroom as a Health Centre, with an enquiry desk where the children can become involved in role-play and discussion. Display leaflets and posters relating to child health and include the vocabulary from this activity.

## ACTIVITY 2

### TAKING MEDICINES

SCIENCE

Medicines

### Learning objectives
To understand that medicines are useful but can be dangerous; to recognise hazards and risks relating to medicines and how to avoid these.

### Resources
An assortment of empty medicine packaging, such as bottles, boxes, blister packs, tubes, and so on; some wrappings from sweets and food to use for comparison; paper, pencils and crayons.

### Activity
Show the children the assortment of different medicine packaging. Examine the items with the children and ask them what might have been in each one. Talk about the ways in which these medicines might be taken, possibly reading the instructions. Which containers held pills or tablets? Are there instructions about taking them? How often were they to be taken? Does it say at what time(s) of day? Which containers held liquid medicine? Which had cream or ointment? Do these containers have special instructions of their own? Draw out the fact that even if the medicines are for children to take, the instructions are for adults to read and they will then supervise the use of all types of medicine.

Explain that although medicines are extremely useful when we are ill, they are drugs not sweets, and can be dangerous if the wrong amounts are taken or used. That is why there are always detailed instructions for adults to read and follow correctly.

Ask the children how they could tell that these packets and bottles contained medicines and not sweets or treats. Talk about the colours and styles used for packaging medicines, and compare them with sweet wrappers and food containers. Explain that the recognisable and sometimes difficult to open packaging helps people, especially children, to understand that they contain not sweets or food but something that could be dangerous if eaten and the instructions not followed carefully. Ask the children why it is dangerous to put medicines in different containers. Point out that young children might mistake a medicine for something nice to eat.

Ask the children to suggest a good place to keep medicines so that they are not accidentally discovered by young children. Remind the children that they should never eat anything unless they know what it is, and that it is safe to eat.

### Recording
Ask the children to compare a container for a medicine with one for sweets or a drink. They could examine and draw each one, writing labels that highlight the differences.

### Differentiation
Children:
■ are aware that medicines can be dangerous and recognise differences between the packaging of medical products and food items
■ understand that medicines can be dangerous, that they are packaged differently from food items and should be kept out of the reach of children
■ understand that medicines can be dangerous; distinguish between medical products and food items; recognise risks and hazards of medicines and how to avoid them.

### Plenary
Remind the children that although medicines are useful in curing a variety of illnesses and help people to get better, they can be very dangerous if people do not use them properly.

CURRICULUM LINKS ages 5–7: Food and healthy eating

## Medicines

The instructions given by the doctor or nurse should be followed carefully. Children should not take any medicines unless they are given to them by a parent or carer.

### Display
Arrange the containers so that the children can become familiar with medical packaging.

## ACTIVITY 3

## ASKING QUESTIONS

SCIENCE

### Learning objective
To ask questions about medicines and health.

### Resources
A health worker or nurse who can talk to the children and is prepared to answer their questions; a camera or video camera (perhaps obtain a video clip of children being treated at a health centre to stimulate questions); cards, paper, pencils.

### Preparation
Arrange for someone to visit the children to talk briefly about health and illness and the use of medicines. Health centres often have people trained to work with young children in this way. Explain the focus of the activity: this might be a topical issue or a more general theme. Suggest an initial talk, then an opportunity for the children to ask questions. Arrange for photographs to be taken, if appropriate.
   Plan this activity in three parts to take place over a number of days:
1. Initiating questions with the children
2. Refining the questions and rehearsing
3. Meeting the visitor.

### Activity
#### Part 1
Tell the children that a visitor will be coming to talk with them about their health, how to stay fit and well, and about medicines they might need to take if they do become ill. Explain who the person is, what his or her job is, and what area of work he or she is an expert in. Ask the children to consider whether there is anything about the topic they are unsure about, anything they would like to know which perhaps the visitor can help to explain. Tell the children to think of questions they might ask the visitor.
   If appropriate, give the children the opportunity to talk to each other in pairs to discuss and decide on ideas for questions. Once they have thought of some ideas, the pairs could then turn these into simple questions.

#### Part 2
Collate the questions as a class. Maybe two questions are similar and should be combined. Others might need more or fewer words to make them suitable. If necessary, guide the children towards asking important questions they have omitted.
   Print out the questions for each child, perhaps on cards, with up to four children sharing a question. Each question can be arranged to allow two to four children to speak.
   Have a simple rehearsal, so that the children are confident and understand when they will be required to speak. Explain that you will introduce the visitor, who will then talk for a few minutes. Tell the children they will need to listen carefully, as the visitor is an expert and whatever s/he will say is important. Then explain that you will introduce the people

asking the questions: *The first question is from Dilip and Sasha. Now Anita and Leon have a question they would like to ask. There is something important Tom and Calli would like to know.* Encourage the children to listen to all of the questions and answers, and not concentrate solely on their own question.

Point out that it is important to thank the person who will be giving their time to help the children. Perhaps arrange for a child to thank the speaker.

If appropriate, hand the speaker a copy of the questions beforehand so s/he has the chance to adapt their introductory talk accordingly.

### Part 3
On the day of the visit, arrange the children so that they are sitting comfortably and can stand up easily when required to ask their question. Eagerly anticipate the visitor's arrival and encourage a friendly welcome. Take photographs, if appropriate.

After the question and answer session, make sure the children participate in thanking the speaker.

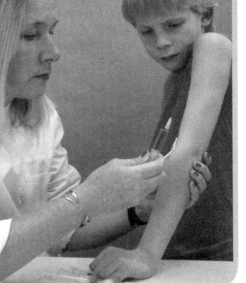

### Recording
The children can write out the answer to their question, either on the reverse of their question card or on a separate piece of paper. Alternatively, they can write an account of the visit that includes their own question and its answer.

### Differentiation
Children:
- with help think of a question relating to health and medicines and take part in a question and answer session with a visitor
- provide ideas for questions about health and medicines, taking part in a question and answer session with a visitor
- provide relevant ideas for questions about health and medicines, taking part confidently in a question and answer session with a visitor.

### Plenary
Comment on how useful the visit by the expert was, how well the children listened and how much you have all learned. Perhaps emphasise some of the new points that were made.

### Display
Provide captions for any photographs taken and display them with any posters, leaflets and so on that the visitor has supplied.

## ACTIVITY 4
# TELLING OTHERS
SCIENCE

### Learning objective
To communicate information about the safe use of medicines.

### Resources
Plain and coloured poster paper, pencils and crayons, glue; board or flip chart.

## 5 Medicines

### Activity
Explain that occasionally young children have accidentally taken medicines and as a result have become very ill. They have swallowed medicines that were not meant for them, possibly mistaking tablets for sweets. Or perhaps the medicines were not kept safely.

Ask the children to think of messages that could be used to remind others that medicines can be harmful if not used properly, and that it is important to avoid this risk. List the children's ideas on the board of flip chart. Their ideas might include: *Do not let children find medicines. Medicines are not sweets. Only take medicines when Mum or Dad or someone responsible tells you. Keep medicines out of children's reach.*

Point out that these slogans could be displayed on an eye-catching poster. Suggest refining any longer messages so that unnecessary words are removed, making the message easier to remember. Also decide to whom each message might be addressed and edit it accordingly. For example, *Lock medicines away safely* would be intended for adults; *Don't touch medicines* would be a message to young children.

Consider illustrations that would be effective on the posters, especially for young children who might not be able to read.

Ask the children to choose a slogan to form their poster, and to think carefully about illustrations they might use. Talk about making the poster simple, bold and attractive so that the message stands out well. Allow the children some time to think about and draft their design, considering where the words will be, how much space is required, where the illustrations will fit and what colours will be used.

Suggest the children write out the words of the message on coloured paper. These can be cut out as cloud/bubble/geometric shapes and glued onto the poster background. This way, mistakes and lack of space on the background can be avoided. Illustrations can then be arranged around the message. Some children might like to invent a cartoon character or depict themselves giving the message in a speech bubble.

### Differentiation
Children:
- with prompting provide ideas and with help design a poster to communicate information about the safe use of medicines
- provide ideas and create a poster to communicate information about the safe use of medicines
- provide ideas and create an effective poster to communicate information about the safe use of medicines.

### Plenary
Display the children's posters and discuss how effective they are. Which ones do the children think do a good job in spreading information about the safe use of medicines? Which ones are aimed at children? Which are to remind adults how to look after medicines safely?

### Display
Arrange the children's posters around the school to demonstrate their importance in passing on information. Perhaps the health centre would also be interested in displaying some.

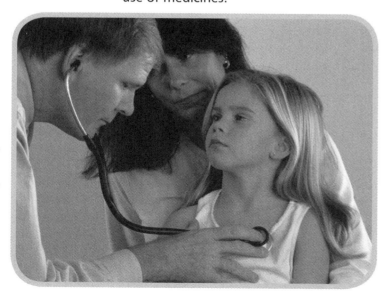

# Growing up

**Section 6**

## FOCUS
### SCIENCE
- animals, including humans, produce young
- caring for babies and toddlers
- comparing the development of babies and young children
- gathering information from a variety of sources

## ACTIVITY 1

### ANIMALS AND THEIR YOUNG

### Learning objective
To know that animals, including humans, produce young which grow up to become adults.

### Resources
Books, pictures and video clips showing a range of adult animals and their young; photocopiable page 59; pencils.

### Preparation
Compile a list of key words for the children to refer to when completing the photocopiable sheet.

### Activity
Start with a quiz in which you give the name of an animal and the children supply the name of the young, for example *cow – calf; hen – chick; cat – kitten; fox – cub*, and so on. Perhaps ask the children to supply some other examples. Use pictures to identify less familiar animals. Point out that all animals have young, but the young of some animals do not have a different name. Earthworms and snails, for example, have young, but we do not seem to have special names for them.

Show the children a picture of a duck and a duckling or a hen and a chick. Ask them if they notice any differences between the young and its parent. What is the main difference? More subtle differences? Explain that many animals are quite similar to their parents when they are young. They are usually smaller and might have some slight differences in appearance, but on the whole they are recognisable as the offspring of their parents. Ask if the children know of any young animals that look totally different from their parents. Remind them of previous work if appropriate, and talk about caterpillars and butterflies/moths, and tadpoles and frogs/toads. Not only do these young animals look totally different from their parents, but their behaviour, such as feeding and moving, is very different too.

© Photodisc, Inc.

CURRICULUM LINKS ages 5–7: Food and healthy eating

**Growing up**

Remind the children that humans are animals. Show a picture of a familiar adult (perhaps yourself) as a child, and discuss some of the changes that take place as a human grows up.

If available, show the children a video clip of some animals with their young.

### Recording
Show the children photocopiable page 59 and ask them to draw lines to connect the parents with the young and add labels to the pictures.

### Differentiation
Children:
■ know that parents have young which in turn grow into adults
■ recognise the young of a range of animals and understand that they, like humans, grow into adults and have young of their own
■ understand that all animals, including humans, have young which grow into adults and then have young of their own.

### Plenary
Remind the children that all animals have young, and that in many cases the young are physically very similar to their parents but smaller. Talk about other creatures producing young that are very different from the adult, but explain that these change as they grow to become like their parents and then have young of their own.

### Display
Arrange labelled pictures of adult animals and their offspring.

## ACTIVITY 2

## BABIES

SCIENCE

### Learning objective
To appreciate that human babies need a lot of care.

### Resources
A range of realistic baby dolls representing both genders and different ethnic origins; doll/baby clothes and equipment; a video showing a baby being cared for; photographs of babies and parents from a variety of cultures; photocopiable page 60; pencils; board or flip chart.

### Preparation
Organise an area of the classroom to represent a nursery where the children can become involved in role-play.

### Activity
Have a doll in a cot or pram near you. Mention there is a baby in the room who is sleeping and should not be disturbed for a while.

Ask the children if anyone has a baby living with them in their house: a new addition, another person belonging to their family. Explain that you are talking about a child who is less than one year old and who hasn't yet learned how to walk. Ask the siblings of babies to share their experiences of living with a baby. What is it like with a baby in the house? Is it peaceful or noisy? Are there a lot of things around the house especially for the baby? Perhaps a pram, a special chair, baby food, clothes and toys. What does the baby spend most of its time doing? What do the parents/carers have to do for the baby? Is it able to feed itself?

Keep itself clean? Go to the toilet by itself? How does the baby communicate with the family? Can the baby do anything for itself? How do the children themselves help with the baby? Do they keep it amused? Perhaps they are able to fetch things the baby needs?

Gently 'wake up' and hold the sleepy 'baby'. Bring other children into the discussion by asking for their experiences of other people's babies. Perhaps a baby lives next door or relatives have babies.

Discuss how a baby needs constant care, and can do very little for itself. Point out that it needs to be kept safe from harm – with no one to look after it the baby would die.

Play a video clip of a baby to show its movements and demonstrate how it is cared for. Show the children pictures of mothers and babies from different cultures. Explain that parents/carers in other countries might not have all the high-tech baby equipment we have, but still care for their babies just as well. Encourage the children to notice differences, such as methods of transporting babies.

Now ask the children to name some familiar baby animals that are looked after by their parents. Talk about puppies, kittens and baby birds. Then explain that there are some animals that do not look after their babies because the young can look after themselves as soon as they are born. These include snails, beetles, earthworms, frogs and butterflies. Point out that, by contrast, human babies need to be looked after 24 hours a day for quite a few years.

Ask the children to help you generate a list of things a human baby can do, such as sleep; make noises, including crying and gurgling; suck, eat, drink; soil a nappy; wave arms and legs; wriggle; smile; play, and so on.

Then list the things a baby cannot do which the children can. Include things such as feed yourself, go to the toilet, talk, walk, read, draw, play outdoor games.

Encourage the children to care for the 'baby' through role-play, perhaps in a corner of the room designated as a nursery.

Growing up

## Recording
Show the children photocopiable page 60, which has an illustration of a number of babies. Ask the children to describe what a baby can do and what a baby cannot yet do. Tell them whether they should make a list or write sentences.

## Differentiation
Children:
■ know that human babies need to be looked after, describing with words some of the things a baby can and cannot do
■ are aware that human babies need to be cared for constantly, describing in sentences things that a baby can and cannot do
■ understand why human babies need to be cared for constantly, describing in detail the things that a baby can and cannot do.

## Plenary
Explain that human babies need constant care because they can do very little for themselves. Perhaps most importantly, they cannot find food and feed themselves. They need an adult to care for them and keep them safe and well.

## Display
Have pictures, photographs and dolls representing human babies, and baby or doll's equipment for the children to examine.

Growing up

ACTIVITY 3

# BABIES BECOME TODDLERS

### Learning objective
To gather information about the development and care of young children.

### Resources
Video clips, pictures and books showing the development and activities of very young children; paper, pencils and crayons.

### Preparation
If appropriate, ask a parent or carer to make a short video of a toddler to show how it behaves and the care that it needs. Let parents/carers with small children know that they might be asked for information. Explain the form the questions will take and how the answers will help the children with their topic work.

### Activity
Begin by showing a video clip or pictures of a toddler. Explain that this child has reached the next stage of growing up. It is no longer a baby, spending its time sleeping and lying in a cot, but has learned to walk and is becoming more independent.

Perhaps some children have a brother or a sister who has reached this stage. Using shared experiences and the information in the video clip, discuss the life of a toddler. What can a child do at this stage? What has changed since it was a baby? What new things is the child learning to do? Now it has learned to walk, does it need looking after in a different way? What does it like to do now? Is it able to play? Can it feed without help yet? What about keeping clean and going to the toilet? Emphasise the changes from baby to toddler, pointing out that the child still needs continual care from an adult. Ask why a toddler should not be left alone. What hasn't it learned yet? Briefly consider some dangers that might befall a toddler who was not looked after constantly.

Ask those children with a toddler in the family to describe what it is like having a very young child in the house. Does the toddler eat the same food as the rest of the family? Is s/he able to join in some games? What does s/he like to do? Does s/he have a favourite toy? What are the things s/he does not like? Do toddlers still sleep during the day? What time do they go to bed? What sort of bed do they need?

Are there any questions that cannot be answered fully? Who could provide the information? Perhaps parents/carers would know the answers, as they are dealing with young children every day. Devise some questions that can be presented to willing parents/carers, who could provide the information required. Perhaps the children want to know what toddlers like to eat. Do all toddlers have the same tastes? What have they learned since they were a baby? What dangers do they have to be protected from? With the help of the children, type and print out the questions requesting information. Arrange for the questionnaires to be distributed to willing parents/carers, with a note suggesting when they should be returned.

## Recording

Ask the children to describe the daily routine of a toddler using drawings and words or sentences. Encourage them to emphasise the care a very young child needs during this stage of its development.

When the replies to the questions are returned, organise some children to collate the information. Pairs of children can focus one question and make a summary or chart of the information, perhaps using word processing or appropriate computer software.

## Differentiation

Children:
- are aware that a baby becomes a toddler who needs to be looked after while it is growing up, recording this with drawings and headings
- recognise some behaviour patterns of a toddler and understand that a very young child needs constant care while it is growing up, recording this with drawings and sentences
- recognise some behaviour patterns of a toddler and show understanding in drawings and sentences why very young children need constant care as they are growing up.

## Plenary

Ask the children to tell you how they would help to care for a toddler who visited them in the classroom. How would they keep him/her occupied? How would they keep him/her safe? Remind the class that very young children need a lot of care from their parents/carers when they are growing up. There are many things they cannot do for themselves, and they have not yet learned about the dangers they are likely to encounter.

## Display

Add pictures of toddlers to the display, with any photographs of the children's siblings.

# ACTIVITY 4

## COMPARING BABIES AND YOUNG CHILDREN

SCIENCE

### Learning objective

To use information acquired to make simple comparisons of babies and young children.

### Resources

Information gathered from the replies to the questions sent to parents/carers in the previous activity; pictures and books showing the development and behaviour of young children; recording sheet; thick paper or card for mounting work; pencils and crayons.

### Preparation

Divide a large sheet of paper into three columns with headings: *baby, toddler, infant*. Prepare a framework for the children's recording (see illustration). Cut pieces of thick paper or card and fold into three parts for mounting the children's work.

### Activity

Point out that the children now know much more about how young children grow up and why they need to be looked after.

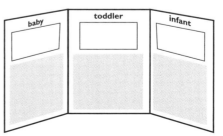

CURRICULUM LINKS ages 5–7: Food and healthy eating

**Growing up**

They have listened to each other sharing experiences, they have watched videos, looked at books and pictures, and have asked questions. Show them the large sheet of paper and point out the three headings. Explain that all the information gathered can be used to compare the different stages of development and behaviour of babies and toddlers and young children like themselves, who are infants.

Perhaps start with feeding. Ask the children to supply the information required. Make notes in the appropriate column to describe what a baby's main food is and how they feed. Similarly, record the toddler's feeding requirements. Then ask the children to compare their own eating habits. For example, they can sit at a table, use cutlery successfully, eat and drink unaided and choose their own food.

Move on to communication. The only noise babies can make is to cry when they need food or attention, but toddlers can make more noises, point and grab. How do the children inform others of their needs?

Consider exercise and play activities, what a baby and toddler can do, and what the children in the class enjoy. Perhaps include favourite toys of each stage of development.

Emphasise the ongoing development from baby to toddler to infant. Point out that the children themselves will continue to develop, learning new skills as they get older. However, they will still need the care of adults throughout their childhood. Human offspring are looked after for many years, until they become adults themselves.

### Recording

Depending on ability and the time available, the children can make an individual record that compares the stages of development of a baby, toddler and themselves. Provide them with a framework for each stage. Encourage them to focus on a particular baby and toddler, and illustrate each stage with a drawing or photograph. They can use themselves as the example of an infant. Then using subheadings such as *feeding, talking/communicating, exercise* and *play*. The children can record information as notes or sentences. Some children might include further comparisons of dress, toys, keeping clean, and so on. Glue the pages to a piece of card folded into three parts and display it appropriately.

Alternatively, children can focus on one or two examples of development, such as feeding and playing. Some children might enjoy continuing this work at home.

### Differentiation

Children:
- use information that has been acquired in a variety of ways to make simple comparisons between a baby, a toddler and themselves, recording this with drawings, headings and words
- using information acquired from a variety of sources, make comparisons between the different stages of child development, recording this with drawings, notes or sentences
- using information acquired from a variety of sources, show comparisons between the different stages of child development, recording this comprehensively with drawings and relevant notes or sentences.

### Plenary

Discuss how the children's work is progressing. Show examples where useful comparisons have been made. Perhaps someone has recorded a new and interesting fact from observation of a baby or toddler, which has not been previously mentioned. Conclude by reminding the children that as a human baby develops and grows, s/he is learning new things and becoming more independent, but s/he still needs the constant care of an adult.

### Display

Arrange the children's work where it can be read and admired.

Growing up

# Animals and their young

_____ _____ _____ _____

_____ _____ _____ _____

_____ _____ _____ _____

_____ _____ _____ _____

CURRICULUM LINKS ages 5–7: Food and healthy eating

# Babies

| What a baby cannot do |
|---|
|  |

| What a baby can do |
|---|
|  |

# Display

It is important to display as much of the children's work as possible. Making their work available for others to see adds value and prestige to what the children have achieved. It also emphasises the importance of the information they have collected, ideas they have had and investigations they have made.

If children know their work will be valued and available for others to see, they will take care over presentation, and the habit of always producing their best efforts is worth encouraging.

## Individual presentation

Collect each child's individual work – drawings, completed worksheets, written pieces, plans, graphs, and so on – and present them in a folder or as a booklet that they can personalise and show to each other and their parents and carers. If necessary, any pieces needed for a classroom display can be photocopied.

Provide photocopies or printouts of texts or photographs, such as fruits and vegetables growing, a recipe, safety information from the health centre, or examples of animals and their young, which the children can include among their own work to give their folders or booklets an extra dimension. Include copies of photographs taken during the activities.

## Classroom display

Begin a display as soon as the work on the topic begins. It will develop as work progresses.

It can be useful to display each child's work relating to a specific activity in a temporary way, perhaps with Blu-Tack, so that discussion and evaluation can take place and the work can be admired. At this stage, make sure the work is displayed where all the children can see it easily. Where appropriate, photocopy and enlarge examples of individual's work to use in a display. If space is limited in the classroom, extend the display into the corridor or school hall.

Frequently refer to the display as the topic develops, reminding the children of the different elements and the progress they are making. Point out links across the different areas.

Look at developing a dictionary/glossary book of relevant vocabulary with pages devoted to groups of associated words, such as adjectives describing appearance, texture and so on of fruits and vegetables, and those relating to different tastes; verbs describing processes; nouns relating to different parts of fruits and vegetables.

## Suggestions for display for each section

The activities in *Food* lend themselves to five separate but linked areas of display, covering *Food*, *Eat more fruits and vegetables*, *Exercise*, *Medicines* and *Growing up*. Ask the children to help with suggestions for appropriate headings, captions and slogans to accompany each display. Discuss colour schemes, ideas for borders and types of lettering, so that the children develop ownership of the displays that show off their work.

### Food (All kinds of food and tasting and eating foods)

■ Where actual foods are displayed, tell the children that they are not for eating.
■ Make important statements a feature, for example *We all need food and water to stay alive*, *We need water to drink and a variety of foods to eat to live healthily*.
■ Group, or arrange as a border, pictures of adults and children following a range of pursuits, and images of popular foods.
■ Arrange the children's work, including any information brought from home.
■ Use packaging, advertising material and fake foods to demonstrate a range of foods. Include real non-perishable foods, such as rice, pasta and dried pulses.
■ Show distinctly the different food groups, perhaps using the circles (section, activity 3).
■ Make labels to describe tastes – salty, sweet, sour and so on (section 2, activity 1) with lists of relevant foods. Display the results of the investigation.

## Display

- Reserve a section of the display to provide information about meals, snacks and treats. Include the children's meal menus.

### Eat more fruit and vegetables
- Build up this display with work and resources from sections 1 to 3.
- This display can be made particularly attractive with images of colourful fruits and vegetables, possibly used as borders or a background.
- Have an area where different fruits and vegetables are named and displayed, perhaps on a daily basis (the fruit/vegetable of the day). Include fresh, dried and tinned examples. If necessary, resort to pictures and packaging, or models that the children can make from Plasticine or a similar material. Tell the children that the real examples are not to be eaten, and advise them whether they can be handled or not.
- To build up a database of as many different fruits and vegetables as possible, create a loose-leaf book, folder or box to which examples can be added as they are discovered. This could be organised alphabetically.
- Use the children's drawings and writing to emphasise the different elements of this work.
- Make a banner, *Eat more fruits and vegetables*, to use as an emphatic heading. Use a bold statement to stress the nutritional importance of fruits and vegetables.
- Set aside an area to present the investigation, practise, and creation of the fruit/vegetable product. Label the safe tools and equipment and make them easily accessible for the children to select. Use posters and children's work that highlight the need for safety, and efficient and hygienic working methods.
- Show the process of the designing and making assignment, from ideas and plans through to the finished product and evaluation. Use photographs as well as drawings to show the finished products.

### Exercise
- Use pictures of children and adults engaged in a wide range of physical activities, perhaps as a border to surround the children's work.
- Highlight vocabulary relating to exercise by printing out appropriate words on coloured strips of paper and scattering these among the children's work.
- Group words relating to different areas of the body with pictures demonstrating methods of exercising these parts.
- Create and display slogans to emphasise how important and enjoyable exercise can be for everyone.
- Reserve an area to indicate the 'before and after' effects of exercise.

### Medicines
- If possible, as a focal point for this section of work, create a small area to resemble a reception/enquiry desk at a health centre.
- Arrange a selection of medicine packaging for the children to examine.
- Display posters and leaflets relating to the safety of medicines, some specially designed for young children, as well as those created by the class.
- Show any photographs taken during the health worker's visit.
- Print out the most relevant questions and answers from the talk, and display them prominently.

### Growing up
- Display a wide range of pictures of animals and their young. The pictures could be presented for the children to match parent with offspring.
- Make a collage of photographs of babies from a variety of cultures.
- Show images of toddlers involved in different activities. Include photographs of the children's siblings, cousins, and so on.
- Make available any relevant information arising from the questionnaire.